THE HISTORY OF PUERTO RICO
BY
R.A. VAN MIDDELDYK

FROM THE SPANISH DISCOVERY TO THE AMERICAN OCCUPATION

EDITED BY MARTIN G. BRUMBAUGH, PH.D., LL.D. PROFESSOR OF PEDAGOGY, UNIVERSITY OF PENNSYLVANIA AND FIRST COMMISSIONER OF EDUCATION FOR PUERTO RICO

EDITOR'S PREFACE

The latest permanent possession of the United States is also the oldest in point of European occupation. The island of Puerto Rico was discovered by Columbus in 1493. It was occupied by the United States Army at Guanica July 25, 1898. Spain formally evacuated the island October 18, 1898, and military government was established until Congress made provision for its control. By act of Congress, approved April 12, 1900, the military control terminated and civil government was formally instituted May 1,1900.

Puerto Rico has an interesting history. Its four centuries under Spanish control is a record of unusual and remarkable events. This record is unknown to the American people. It has never been written satisfactorily in the Spanish language, and not at all in the English language. The author of this volume is the first to give to the reader of English a record of Spanish rule in this "pearl of the Antilles." Mr. Van Middeldyk is the librarian of the Free Public Library of San Juan, an institution created under American civil control. He has had access to all data obtainable in the island, and has faithfully and conscientiously woven this data into a connected narrative, thus giving the reader a view of the social and institutional life of the island for four hundred years.

The author has endeavored to portray salient characteristics of the life on the island, to describe the various acts of the reigning government, to point out the evils of colonial rule, and to figure the general historical and geographical conditions in a manner that enables the reader to form a fairly accurate judgment of the past and present state of Puerto Rico.

No attempt has been made to speculate upon the setting of this record in the larger record of Spanish life. That is a work for the future. But enough history of Spain and in general of continental Europe is given to render intelligible the various and varied governmental activities exercised by Spain in the island. There is, no doubt, much omitted that future research may reveal, and yet it is just to state that the record is fairly continuous, and that no salient factors in the island's history have been overlooked.

The people of Puerto Rico were loyal and submissive to their parent government. No record of revolts and excessive rioting is recorded. The island has been continuously profitable to Spain. With even ordinarily fair administration of government the people have been self-supporting, and in many cases have rendered substantial aid to other Spanish possessions. Her native life—the Boriquén Indians—rapidly became extinct, due to the "gold fever" and the intermarriage of races. The peon class has always been a faithful laboring class in the coffee, sugar, and tobacco estates, and the slave element was never large. A few landowners and the professional classes dominate the island's life. There is no middle class. There is an utter absence of the legitimate fruits of democratic institutions. The poor are in every way objects of pity and of sympathy. They are the hope of the island. By education, widely diffused, a great unrest will ensue, and from this unrest will come the social, moral, and civic uplift of the people.

These people do not suffer from the lack of civilization. They suffer from the

3

kind of civilization they have endured. The life of the people is static. Her institutions and customs are so set upon them that one is most impressed with the absence of legitimate activities. The people are stoically content. Such, at least, was the condition in 1898. Under the military government of the United States much was done to prepare the way for future advance. Its weakness was due to its effectiveness. It did for the people what they should learn to do for themselves. The island needed a radically new governmental activity—an activity that would develop each citizen into a self-respecting and self-directing force in the island's uplift. This has been supplied by the institution of civil government. The outlook of the people is now infinitely better than ever before. The progress now being made is permanent. It is an advance made by the people for themselves. Civil government is the fundamental need of the island.

Under civil government the entire reorganization of the life of the people is being rapidly effected. The agricultural status of the island was never so hopeful. The commercial activity is greatly increased. The educational awakening is universal and healthy. Notwithstanding the disastrous cyclone of 1898, and the confusion incident to a radical governmental reorganization, the wealth per capita has increased, the home life is improved, and the illiteracy of the people is being rapidly lessened.

President McKinley declared to the writer that it was his desire "to put the conscience of the American people into the islands of the sea." This has been done. The result is apparent. Under wise and conservative guidance by the American executive officers, the people of Puerto Rico have turned to this Republic with a patriotism, a zeal, an enthusiasm that is, perhaps, without a parallel.

In 1898, under President McKinley as commander-in-chief, the army of the United States forcibly invaded this island. This occupation, by the treaty of Paris, became permanent. Congress promptly provided civil government for the island, and in 1901 this conquered people, almost one million in number, shared in the keen grief that attended universally the untimely death of their conqueror. The island on the occasion of the martyr's death was plunged in profound sorrow, and at a hundred memorial services President McKinley was mourned by thousands, and he was tenderly characterized as "the founder of human liberty in Puerto Rico."

The judgment of the American people relative to this island is based upon meager data. The legal processes attending its entrance into the Union have been the occasion of much comment. This comment has invariably lent itself to a discussion of the effect of judicial decision upon our home institutions. It has been largely a speculative concern. In some cases it has become a political concern in the narrowest partisan sense. The effect of all this upon the people of Puerto Rico has not been considered. Their rights and their needs have not come to us. We have not taken President McKinley's broad, humane, and exalted view of our obligation to these people. They have implicitly entrusted their life, liberty, and property to our guardianship. The great Republic has a debt of honor to the island which indifference and ignorance of its needs can never pay. It is hoped that this record of their struggles during four centuries will be a welcome source of insight and guidance to the people of the United States in their efforts to see their duty and do it.

M. G. BRUMBAUGH. PHILADELPHIA, *January 1, 1903.*

AUTHOR'S PREFACE

Some years ago, Mr. Manuel Elzaburu, President of the San Juan Provincial Atheneum, in a public speech, gave it as his opinion that the modern historian of Puerto Rico had yet to appear. This was said, not in disparagement of the island's only existing history, but rather as a confirmation of the general opinion that the book which does duty as such is incorrect and incomplete.

This book is Friar Iñigo Abbad's Historia de la Isla San Juan Bautista, which was written in 1782 by disposition of the Count of Floridablanca, the Minister of Colonies of Charles III, and published in Madrid in 1788. In 1830 it was reproduced in San Juan without any change in the text, and in 1866 Mr. José Julian Acosta published a new edition with copious notes, comments, and additions, which added much data relative to the Benedictine monks, corrected numerous errors, and supplemented the chapters, some of which, in the original, are exceedingly short, the whole history terminating abruptly with the nineteenth chapter, that is, with the beginning of the eighteenth century. The remaining 21 chapters are merely descriptive of the country and people.

Besides this work there are others by Puerto Rican authors, each one elucidating one or more phases of the island's history. With these separate and diverse materials, supplemented by others of my own, I have constructed the present history.

The transcendental change in the island's social and political conditions, inaugurated four years ago, made the writing of an English history of Puerto Rico necessary. The American officials who are called upon to guide the destinies and watch over the moral, material, and intellectual progress of the inhabitants of this new accession to the great Republic will be able to do so all the better when they have a knowledge of the people's historical antecedents.

I have endeavored to supply this need to the best of my ability, and herewith offer to the public the results of an arduous, though self-imposed task.

R.A.V.M.

SAN JUAN, PUERTO RICO, *November 3, 1902.*

PART I HISTORICAL
CHAPTER I THE DEPARTURE

1493

Eight centuries of a gigantic struggle for supremacy between the Crescent and the Cross had devastated the fairest provinces of the Spanish Peninsula. Boabdil, the last of the Moorish kings, had delivered the keys of Granada into the hands of Queen Isabel, the proud banner of the united kingdoms of Castile and Aragon floated triumphant from the walls of the Alhambra, and Providence, as if to recompense Iberian knighthood for turning back the tide of Moslem conquest, which threatened to overrun the whole of meridional Europe, had laid a new world, with all its inestimable treasures and millions of benighted inhabitants, at the feet of the Catholic princes.

Columbus had just returned from his first voyage. He had been scorned as an adventurer by the courtiers of Lisbon, mocked as a visionary by the learned priests of the Council in Salamanca, who, with texts from the Scriptures and quotations from the saints, had tried to convince him that the world was flat; he had been pointed at by the rabble in the streets as a madman who maintained that there was a land where the people walked with their heads down; and, after months of trial, he had been able to equip his three small craft and collect a crew of ninety men only by the aid of a royal schedule offering exemption from punishment for offenses against the laws to all who should join the expedition.

At last he had sailed amid the murmurs of an incredulous crowd, who thought him and his companions doomed to certain destruction, and now he had returned[1] bringing with him the living proofs of what he had declared to exist beyond that mysterious ocean, and showed to the astounded people samples of the unknown plants and animals, and of *the gold* which he had said would be found there in fabulous quantities.

It was the proudest moment of the daring navigator's life when, clad in his purple robe of office, bedecked with the insignia of his rank, he entered the throne-room of the palace in Barcelona and received permission to be seated in the royal presence to relate his experiences. Around the hall stood the grandees of Spain and the magnates of the Church, as obsequious and attentive to him now as they had been proud and disdainful when, a hungry wanderer, he had knocked at the gates of La Rabida to beg bread for his son. It was the acme of the discoverer's destiny, the realization of his dream of glory, the well-earned recompense of years of persevering endeavor.

The news of the discovery created universal enthusiasm. When it was announced that a second expedition was being organized there was no need of a royal schedule of remission of punishment to criminals to obtain crews. The Admiral's residence was besieged all day long by the hidalgos[2] who were anxious to share with him the expected glories and riches. The cessation of hostilities in Granada had left thousands of knights, whose only patrimony was their sword, without occupation—men with iron muscles, inured to hardship and danger, eager for adventure and conquest.

Then there were the monks and priests, whose religious zeal was stimulated by the prospect of converting to Christianity the benighted inhabitants of unknown realms; there were ruined traders, who hoped to mend their fortunes with the gold to be had, as they thought, for picking it up; finally, there were the protégés of royalty and of influential persons at court, who aspired to lucrative places in the new territories; in short, the Admiral counted among the fifteen hundred companions of his second expedition individuals of the bluest blood in Spain.

As for the mariners, men-at-arms, mechanics, attendants, and servants, they were mostly greedy, vicious, ungovernable, and turbulent adventurers.[3]

The confiscated property of the Jews, supplemented by a loan and some extra duties on articles of consumption, provided the funds for the expedition; a sufficient quantity of provisions was embarked; twenty Granadian lancers with their spirited Andalusian horses were accommodated; cuirasses, swords, pikes, crossbows, muskets, powder and balls were ominously abundant; seed-corn, rice, sugar-cane, vegetables, etc., were not forgotten; cattle, sheep, goats, swine, and fowls for stocking the new provinces, provided for future needs; and a breed of mastiff dogs, originally intended, perhaps, as watch-dogs only, but which became in a short time the dreaded destroyers of natives. Finally, Pope Alexander VI, of infamous memory, drew a line across the map of the world, from pole to pole,[4] and assigned all the undiscovered lands west of it to Spain, and those east of it to Portugal, thus arbitrarily dividing the globe between the two powers.

At daybreak, September 25, 1493, seventeen ships, three carácas of one hundred tons each, two naos, and twelve caravels, sailed from Cadiz amid the ringing of bells and the enthusiastic Godspeeds of thousands of spectators. The son of a Genoese wool-carder stood there, the equal in rank of the noblest hidalgo in Spain, Admiral of the Indian Seas, Viceroy of all the islands and continents to be discovered, and one-tenth of all the gold and treasures they contained would be his!

Alas for the evanescence of worldly greatness! All this glory was soon to be eclipsed. Eight years after that day of triumph he again landed on the shore of Spain a pale and emaciated prisoner in chains.

It may easily be conceived that the voyage for these fifteen hundred men, most of whom were unaccustomed to the sea, was not a pleasure trip.

Fortunately they had fine weather and fair wind till October 26th, when they experienced their first tropical rain and thunder-storm, and the Admiral ordered litanies. On November 2d he signaled to the fleet to shorten sail, and on the morning of the 3d fifteen hundred pairs of wondering eyes beheld the mountains of an island mysteriously hidden till then in the bosom of the Atlantic Ocean.

Among the spectators were Bernal Diaz de Pisa, accountant of the fleet, the first conspirator in America; thirteen Benedictine friars, with Boil at their head, who, with Morén Pedro de Margarit, the strategist, respectively represented the religious and military powers; there was Roldán, another insubordinate, the first alcalde of the Española; there were Alonzo de Ojeda and Guevára, true knights-errant, who were soon to distinguish themselves: the first by the capture of the chief Caonabó, the second by his romantic love-affair with Higuemota, the daughter of the chiefess Anacaóna. There was Adrian Mojíca, destined shortly to be hanged on the ramparts of Fort Concepción by order of the Viceroy. There was Juan de Esquivél, the future conqueror of Jamaica; Sebastian Olano, receiver of the royal share of the gold and other riches that no one doubted to find; Father Marchena, the Admiral's first protector, friend, and counselor; the two knight commanders of military orders Gallego and Arroyo; the fleet's physician, Chanca; the queen's three servants, Navarro, Peña-soto, and Girau; the pilot, Antonio de Torres, who was to return to Spain with the Admiral's ship and first despatches. There was Juan de la Cosa, cartographer, who traced the first map of the Antilles; there were the father and uncle of Bartolomé de las Casas, the apostle of the Indies; Diego de Peñalosa, the first notary public; Fermin Jedo, the metallurgist, and Villacorta, the mechanical engineer. Luis de Ariega, afterward famous as the defender of the fort at Magdalena; Diego Velasquez, the future conqueror of Cuba; Vega, Abarca, Gil Garcia, Marguéz, Maldonado, Beltrán and many other doughty warriors, whose names had been the terror of the Moors during the war in Granada. Finally, there were Diego Columbus, the Admiral's brother; and among the men-at-arms, one, destined to play the principal rôle in the conquest of Puerto Rico. His name was Juan Ponce, a native of Santervas or Sanservas de Campos in the kingdom of Leon. He had served fifteen years in the war with the Moors as page or shield-bearer to Pedro Nuñez de Guzman, knight commander of the order of Calatráva, and he had joined Columbus like the rest —to seek his fortune in the western hemisphere.

FOOTNOTES:

[Footnote 1: March 15, 1493.]

[Footnote 2: Literally, "*hijos d'algo*," sons of something or somebody.]

[Footnote 3: La Fuente. Hista. general de España.]

[Footnote 4: Along the 30th parallel of longitude W. of Greenwich.]

CHAPTER II
THE DISCOVERY
1493

THE first island discovered on this voyage lies between 14° and 15° north latitude, near the middle of a chain of islands of different sizes, intermingled with rocks and reefs, which stretches from Trinidad, near the coast of Venezuela, in a north-by-westerly direction to Puerto Rico. They are divided in two groups, the Windward Islands forming the southern, the Leeward Islands the northern portion of the chain.

The Admiral shaped his course in the direction in which the islands, one after the other, loomed up, merely touching at some for the purpose of obtaining what information he could, which was meager enough.

For an account of the expedition's experiences on that memorable voyage, we have the fleet physician Chanca's circumstantial description addressed to the Municipal Corporation of Seville, sent home by the same pilot who conveyed the Admiral's first despatches to the king and queen.

After describing the weather experienced up to the time the fleet arrived at the island "de Hierro," he tells their worships that for nineteen or twenty days they had the best weather ever experienced on such a long voyage, excepting on the eve of San Simon, when they had a storm which for four hours caused them great anxiety.

At daybreak on Sunday, November 3d, the pilot of the flagship announced land. "It was marvelous," says Chanca, "to see and hear the people's manifestations of joy; and with reason, for they were very weary of the hardships they had undergone, and longed to be on land again."

The first island they saw was high and mountainous. As the day advanced they saw another more level, and then others appeared, till they counted six, some of good size, and all covered with forest to the water's edge.

Sailing along the shore of the first discovered island for the distance of a league, and finding no suitable anchoring ground, they proceeded to the next island, which was four or five leagues distant, and here the Admiral landed, bearing the royal standard, and took formal possession of this and all adjacent lands in the name of their Highnesses. He named the first island Dominica, because it was discovered on a Sunday, and to the second island he gave the name of his ship, Marie-Galante.

"In this island," says Chanca, "it was wonderful to see the dense forest and the great variety of unknown trees, some in bloom, others with fruit, everything looking so green. We found a tree the leaves whereof resembled laurel leaves, but not so large, and they exhaled the finest odor of cloves.[5]

"There were fruits of many kinds, some of which the men imprudently tasted, with the result that their faces swelled, and that they suffered such violent pain in throat and mouth[6] that they behaved like madmen, the application of cold substances giving them some relief." No signs of inhabitants were discovered, so they remained ashore two hours only and left next morning early (November 4th) in the direction of another island seven or eight leagues northward. They anchored off the southernmost coast of it, now known as Basse Terre, and admired a mountain in the distance, which seemed to reach into the sky (the volcano "la Souffrière"), and the beautiful waterfall on its flank. The Admiral sent a small caravel close inshore to look for a port, which was soon found. Perceiving some huts, the captain landed, but the people who occupied them escaped into the forest as soon as they saw the strangers. On entering the huts they found two large parrots (guacamayos) entirely different from those seen until then by the Spaniards, much cotton, spun and ready for spinning, and other articles, bringing away a little of each, "especially," says the doctor, "four or five bones of human arms and legs."

From this the Admiral concluded that he had found the islands inhabited by the redoubtable Caribs, of whom he had heard on his first voyage, and who were said to eat human flesh. The general direction in which these islands were situated had been pointed out to him by the natives of Guanahani and the Española; hence, he had steered a southwesterly course on this his second voyage, "and," says the doctor, "by the goodness of God and the Admiral's knowledge, we came as straight as if we had come by a known and continuous route."

Having found a convenient port and seen some groups of huts, the inhabitants of which fled as soon as they perceived the ships, the Admiral gave orders that the next morning early parties of men should go on shore to reconnoiter. Accordingly some captains, each with a small band of men, dispersed. Most of them returned before noon with the tangible results of their expeditions; one party brought a boy of about fourteen years of age, who, from the signs he made, was understood to be a captive from some other island; another party brought a child that had been abandoned by the man who was leading it by the hand when he perceived the Spaniards; others had taken some women; and one party was accompanied by women who had voluntarily joined them and who, on that

9

account, were believed to be captives also. Captain Diego Marquiz with six men, who had entered the thickest part of the forest, did not return that night, nor the three following days, notwithstanding the Admiral had sent Alonzo de Ojeda with forty men to explore the jungle, blow trumpets, and do all that could be done to find them. When, on the morning of the fourth day, they had not returned, there was ground for concluding that they had been killed and eaten by the natives; but they made their appearance in the course of the day, emaciated and wearied, having suffered great hardships, till by chance they had struck the coast and followed it till they reached the ships. They brought ten persons, with them— women and boys.

During the days thus lost the other captains collected more than twenty female captives, and three boys came running toward them, evidently escaping from their captors. Few men were seen. It was afterward ascertained that ten canoes full had gone on one of their marauding expeditions. In their different expeditions on shore the Spaniards found all the huts and villages abandoned, and in them "an infinite quantity" of human bones and skulls hanging on the walls as receptacles. From the natives taken on board the Spaniards learned that the name of the first island they had seen was Cayri or Keiree; the one they were on they named Sibuqueira, and they spoke of a third, not yet discovered, named Aye-Aye. The Admiral gave to Sibuqueira the name of Guadaloupe.

Anchors were weighed at daybreak on November 10th. About noon of the next day the fleet reached an island which Juan de la Cosa laid down on his map with the name Santa Maria de Monserrat. From the Indian women on board it was understood that this island had been depopulated by the Caribs and was then uninhabited. On the same day in the afternoon they made another island which, according to Navarrete, was named by the Admiral Santa Maria de la Redonda (the round one), and seeing that there were many shallows in the neighborhood, and that it would be dangerous to continue the voyage during the night, the fleet came to anchor.

On the following morning (the 13th) another island was discovered (la Antigua); thence the fleet proceeded in a northwesterly direction to San Martin, without landing at any place, because, as Chanca observes, "the Admiral was anxious to arrive at 'la Española.'"

After weighing anchor at San Martin on the morning of Thursday the 14th, the fleet experienced rough weather and was driven southward, anchoring the same day off the island Aye-Aye (Santa Cruz).

Fernandez, the Admiral's son, in his description of his father's second voyage, says that a small craft (a sloop) with twenty-five men was sent ashore to take some of the people, that Columbus might obtain information from them regarding his whereabouts. While they carried out this order a canoe with four men, two women, and a boy approached the ships, and, struck with astonishment at what they saw, they never moved from one spot till the sloop returned with four kidnaped women and three children.

When the natives in the canoe saw the sloop bearing down upon them, and that they had no chance of escape, they showed fight. Two Spaniards were wounded

—an arrow shot by one of the amazons went clear through a buckler—then the canoe was overturned, and finding a footing in a shallow place, they continued the fight till they were all taken, one of them being mortally wounded by the thrust of a lance.

To regain the latitude in which he was sailing when the storm began to drive his ships southwestward to Aye-Aye, the Admiral, after a delay of only a few hours, steered north, until, toward nightfall, he reached a numerous group of small islands. Most of them appeared bare and devoid of vegetation. The next morning (November 15th) a small caravel was sent among the group to explore, the other ships standing out to sea for fear of shallows, but nothing of interest was found except a few Indian fishermen. All the islands were uninhabited, and they were baptized "the eleven thousand Virgins." The largest one, according to Navarrete, was named Santa Ursula—"la Virgin Gorda" (the fat Virgin) according to Angleria.

During the night the ships lay to at sea. On the 16th the voyage was continued till the afternoon of the 17th, when another island was sighted; the fleet sailed along its southern shore for a whole day. That night two women and a boy of those who had voluntarily joined the expedition in Sobuqueira, swam ashore, having recognized their home. On the 19th the fleet anchored in a bay on the western coast, where Columbus landed and took possession in the name of his royal patrons with the same formalities as observed in Marie-Galante, and named the island San Juan Bautista. Near the landing-place was found a deserted village consisting of a dozen huts of the usual size surrounding a larger one of superior construction; from the village a road or walk, hedged in by trees and plants, led to the sea, "which," says Muñoz,[7] "gave it the aspect of some cacique's place of seaside recreation."

After remaining two days in port (November 20th and 21st), and without a single native having shown himself, the fleet lifted anchor on the morning of the 22d, and proceeding on its northwesterly course, reached the bay of Samaná, in Española, before night, whence, sailing along the coast, the Admiral reached the longed-for port of Navidad on the 25th, only to find that the first act of the bloody drama that was to be enacted in this bright new world had already been performed.

Here we leave Columbus and his companions to play the important rôles in the conquest of America assigned to each of them. The fortunes of the yeoman of humble birth, the former lance-bearer or stirrup-page of the knight commander of Calatráva, already referred to, were destined to become intimately connected with those of the island whose history we will now trace.

FOOTNOTES:

[Footnote 5: The "Caryophyllus pimienta," Coll y Toste.]

[Footnote 6: Navarrete supposes this to have been the fruit of the Manzanilla "hippomane Mancinella," which produces identical effects.]

[Footnote 7: Historia del Nuevo Mundo.]

CHAPTER III
PONCE AND CERON
1500-1511

Friar Iñigo Abbad, in his History of the Island San Juan Bautista de Puerto Rico, gives the story of the discovery in a very short chapter, and terminates it with the words: "Columbus sailed for Santo Domingo November 22, 1493, and thought no more of the island, which remained forgotten till Juan Ponce returned to explore it in 1508."

This is not correct. The island was not forgotten, for Don José Julian de Acosta, in his annotations to the Benedictine monk's history (pp. 21 and 23), quotes a royal decree of March 24, 1505, appointing Vicente Yañez Pinzón Captain and "corregidor" of the island San Juan Bautista and governor of the fort that he was to construct therein. Pinzón transferred his rights and titles in the appointment to Martin Garcia de Salazar, in company with whom he stocked the island with cattle; but it seems that Boriquén did not offer sufficient scope for the gallant pilot's ambition, for we find him between the years 1506 and 1508 engaged in seeking new conquests on the continent.

As far as Columbus himself is concerned, the island was certainly forgotten amid the troubles that beset him on all sides almost from the day of his second landing in "la Española." From 1493 to 1500 a series of insurrections broke out, headed successively by Diaz, Margarit, Aguado, Roldán, and others, supported by the convict rabble that, on the Admiral's own proposals to the authorities in Spain, had been liberated from galleys and prisons on condition that they should join him on his third expedition. These men, turbulent, insubordinate, and greedy, found hunger, hardships, and sickness where they had expected to find plenty, comfort, and wealth. The Admiral, who had indirectly promised them these things, to mitigate the universal and bitter disappointment, had recourse to the unwarrantable expedients of enslaving the natives, sending them to Spain to be sold, of levying tribute on those who remained, and, worst of all, dooming them to a sure and rapid extermination by forced labor.

The natives, driven to despair, resisted, and in the encounters between the naked islanders and the mailed invaders Juan Ponce distinguished himself so that Nicolas de Ovando, the governor, made him the lieutenant of Juan Esquivél, who was then engaged in "pacifying" the province of Higüey.[8] After Esquivél's departure on the conquest of Jamaica, Ponce was advanced to the rank of captain, and it was while he was in the Higüey province that he learned from the Boriquén natives, who occasionally visited the coast, that there was gold in the rivers of their as yet unexplored island. This was enough to awaken his ambition to explore it, and having asked permission of Ovando, it was granted.

Ponce equipped a caravel at once, and soon after left the port of Salvaleon with a few followers and some Indians to serve as guides and interpreters (1508).

They probably landed at or near the same place at which their captain had landed fifteen years before with the Admiral, that is to say, in the neighborhood of la Aguáda, where, according to Las Casas, the ships going and coming to and from Spain had called regularly to take in fresh water ever since the year 1502.

12

The strangers were hospitably received. It appears that the mother of the local cacique, who was also the chief cacique of that part of the island, was a woman of acute judgment. She had, no doubt, heard from fugitives from la Española of the doings of the Spaniards there, and of their irresistible might in battle, and had prudently counseled her son to receive the intruders with kindness and hospitality.

Accordingly Ponce and his men were welcomed and feasted. They were supplied with provisions; areitos (dances) were held in their honor; batos (games of ball) were played to amuse them, and the practise, common among many of the aboriginal tribes in different parts of the world, of exchanging names with a visitor as a mark of brotherly affection, was also resorted to to cement the new bonds of friendship, so that Guaybána became Ponce for the time being, and Ponce Guaybána. The sagacious mother of the chief received the name of Doña Inéz, other names were bestowed on other members of the family, and to crown all, Ponce received the chief's sister in marriage.

Under these favorable auspices Ponce made known his desire to see the places where the chiefs obtained the yellow metal for the disks which, as a distinctive of their rank, they wore as medals round their neck. Guaybána responded with alacrity to his Spanish brother's wish, and accompanied him on what modern gold-seekers would call "a prospecting tour" to the interior. The Indian took pride in showing him the rivers Manatuabón, Manatí, Sibucó, and others, and in having their sands washed in the presence of his white friends, little dreaming that by so doing he was sealing the doom of himself and people.

Ponce was satisfied with the result of his exploration, and returned to la Española in the first months of 1509, taking with him the samples of gold collected, and leaving behind some of his companions, who probably then commenced to lay the foundations of Capárra. It is believed that Guaybána accompanied him to see and admire the wonders of the Spanish settlement. The gold was smelted and assayed, and found to be 450 maravedis per peso fine, which was not as fine as the gold obtained in la Española, but sufficiently so for the king of Spain's purposes, for he wrote to Ponce in November, 1509: "I have seen your letter of August 16th. Be very diligent in searching for gold mines in the island of San Juan; take out as much as possible, and after smelting it in la Española, send it immediately."

On August 14th of the same year Don Fernando had already written to the captain thanking him for his diligence in the settlement of the island and appointing him governor *ad interim*.

Ponce returned to San Juan in July or the beginning of August, after the arrival in la Española of Diego, the son of Christopher Columbus, with his family and a new group of followers, as Viceroy and Admiral. The Admiral, aware of the part which Ponce had taken in the insurrection of Roldán against his father's authority, bore him no good-will, notwithstanding the king's favorable disposition toward the captain, as manifested in the instructions which he received from Ferdinand before his departure from Spain (May 13, 1509), in which his Highness referred to Juan Ponce de Leon as being by his special grace and good-will authorized to settle the island of San Juan Bautista, requesting the Admiral to make no

13

innovations in the arrangement, and charging him to assist and favor the captain in his undertaking.

After Don Diego's arrival in la Española he received a letter from the king, dated September 15, 1509, saying, "Ovando wrote that Juan Ponce had not gone to settle the island of San Juan for want of stores; now that they have been provided in abundance, let it be done."

But the Admiral purposely ignored these instructions. He deposed Ponce and appointed Juan Ceron as governor in his place, with a certain Miguel Diaz as High Constable, and Diego Morales for the office next in importance. His reason for thus proceeding in open defiance of the king's orders, independent of his resentment against Ponce, was the maintenance of the prerogatives of his rank as conceded to his father, of which the appointment of governors and mayors over any or all the islands discovered by him was one.

Ceron and his two companions, with more than two hundred Spaniards, sailed for San Juan in 1509, and were well received by Guaybána and his Indians, among whom they took up their residence and at once commenced the search for gold. In the meantime Ponce, in his capacity as governor *ad interim*, continued his correspondence with the king, who, March 2, 1510, signed his appointment as permanent governor.[9] This conferred upon him the power to sentence in civil and criminal affairs, to appoint and remove alcaldes, constables, etc., subject to appeal to the government of la Española. Armed with his new authority, and feeling himself strong in the protection of his king, Ponce now proceeded to arrest Ceron and his two fellow officials, and sent them to Spain in a vessel that happened to call at the island, confiscating all their property.

Diego Columbus, on hearing of Ponce's highhanded proceedings, retaliated by the confiscation of all the captain's property in la Española.

These events did not reach the king's ears till September, 1510. He comprehended at once that his protégé had acted precipitately, and gave orders that the three prisoners should be set at liberty immediately after their arrival in Spain and proceed to the Court to appear before the Council of Indies. He next ordered Ponce (November 26, 1510) to place the confiscated properties and Indians of Ceron and his companions at the disposal of the persons they should designate for that purpose. Finally, after due investigation and recognition of the violence of Ponce's proceedings, the king wrote to him June 6, 1511: "Because it has been resolved in the Council of Indies that the government of this and the other islands discovered by his father belongs to the Admiral and his successors, it is necessary to return to Ceron, Diaz, and Morales their staffs of office. You will come to where I am, leaving your property in good security, and We will see wherein we can employ you in recompense of your good services."

Ceron and his companions received instructions not to molest Ponce nor any of his officers, nor demand an account of their acts, and they were recommended to endeavor to gain their good-will and assistance. The reinstated officers returned to San Juan in the latter part of 1511. Ponce, in obedience to the king's commands, quietly delivered the staff of office to Ceron, and withdrew to his residence in Capárra. He had already collected considerable wealth, which was

14

soon to serve him in other adventurous enterprises.

FOOTNOTES:

[Footnote 8: The slaughter of rebellious Indians was called "pacification" by the Spaniards.]

[Footnote 9: The document is signed by Ferdinand and his daughter, Doña Juana, as heir to her mother, for the part corresponding to each in the sovereignty over the island San Juan Bautista.]

CHAPTER IV
FIRST DISTRIBUTION OF INDIANS. "REPARTIMIENTOS"
1510

Soon after Ponce's return from la Española Guaybána sickened and died. Up to this time the harmony established by the prudent cacique between his tribesmen and the Spaniards on their first arrival had apparently not been disturbed. There is no record of any dissension between them during Ponce's absence.

The cacique was succeeded by his brother, who according to custom assumed the name of the deceased chief, together with his authority.

The site for his first settlement, chosen by Ponce, was a low hill in the center of a small plain surrounded by hills, at the distance of a league from the sea, the whole space between being a swamp, "which," says Oviedo, "made the transport of supplies very difficult." Here the captain commenced the construction of a fortified house and chapel, or hermitage, and called the place Capárra.[10]

Among the recently arrived Spaniards there was a young man of aristocratic birth named Christopher de Soto Mayor, who possessed powerful friends at Court. He had been secretary to King Philip I, and according to Abbad, was intended by Ferdinand as future governor of San Juan; but Señor Acosta, the friar's commentator, remarks with reason, that it is not likely that the king, who showed so much tact and foresight in all his acts, should place a young man without experience over an old soldier like Ponce, for whom he had a special regard.

The young hidalgo seemed to aspire to nothing higher than a life of adventure, for he agreed to go as Ponce's lieutenant and form a settlement on the south coast of the island near the bay of Guánica.

"In this settlement," says Oviedo, "there were so many mosquitoes that they alone were enough to depopulate it, and the people passed to Aguáda, which is said to be to the west-nor'-west, on the borders of the river Culebrinas, in the district now known as Aguáda and Aguadilla; to this new settlement they gave the name Sotomayor, and while they were there the Indians rose in rebellion one Friday in the beginning of the year 1511."

* * * * *

The second Guaybána[11] was far from sharing his predecessor's good-will toward the Spaniards or his prudence in dealing with them; nor was the conduct of the newcomers toward the natives calculated to cement the bonds of friendship.

Fancying themselves secure in the friendly disposition of the natives, prompted

15

by that spirit of reckless daring and adventure that distinguished most of the followers of Columbus, anxious to be first to find a gold-bearing stream or get possession of some rich piece of land, they did not confine themselves to the two settlements formed, but spread through the interior, where they began to lay out farms and to work the auriferous river sands.

In the beginning the natives showed themselves willing enough to assist in these labors, but when the brutal treatment to which the people of la Española had been subjected was meted out to them also, and the greed of gold caused their self-constituted masters to exact from them labors beyond their strength, the Indians murmured, then protested, at last they resisted, and at each step the taskmasters became more exacting, more relentless.

At the time of the arrival of the Spaniards the natives of Boriquén seem to have led an Arcadian kind of existence; their bows and arrows were used only when some party of Caribs came to carry off their young men and maidens. Among themselves they lived at peace, and passed their days in lazily swinging in their hammocks and playing ball or dancing their "areytos." With little labor the cultivation of their patches of yucca[12] required was performed by the women, and beyond the construction of their canoes and the carving of some battle club, they knew no industry, except, perhaps, the chipping of some stone into the rude likeness of a man, or of one of the few animals they knew.

These creatures were suddenly called upon to labor from morning to night, to dig and delve, and to stand up to their hips in water washing the river sands. They were forced to change their habits and their food, and from free and, in their own way, happy masters of the soil they became the slaves of a handful of ruthless men from beyond the sea. When Ponce's order to distribute them among his men confirmed the hopelessness of their slavery, they looked upon the small number of their destroyers and began to ask themselves if there were no means of getting rid of them.

* * * * *

The system of "repartimientos" (distribution), sometimes called "encomiendas" (patronage), was first introduced in la Española by Columbus and sanctioned later by royal authority. Father Las Casas insinuates that Ponce acted arbitrarily in introducing it in Boriquén, but there were precedents for it.

The first tribute imposed by Columbus on the natives of la Española was in gold and in cotton[13](1495). Recognizing that the Indians could not comply with this demand, the Admiral modified it, but still they could not satisfy him, and many, to escape the odious imposition, fled to the woods and mountains or wandered about from place to place. The Admiral, in virtue of the powers granted to him, had divided the land among his followers according to rank, or merit, or caprice, and in the year 1496 substituted the forced labor of the Indians for the tribute, each cacique being obliged to furnish a stipulated number of men to cultivate the lands granted. Bobadilla, the Admiral's successor, made this obligation to work on the land extend to the mines, and in the royal instructions given to Ovando, who succeeded Bobadilla, these abuses were confirmed, and he was expressly charged to see to it "that the Indians were employed in collecting

16

gold and other metals for the Castilians, in cultivating their lands, in constructing their houses, and in obeying their commands." The pretext for these abuses was, that by thus bringing the natives into immediate contact with their masters they would be easier converted to Christianity. It is true that the royal ordinances stipulated that the Indians should be well treated, and be paid for their work like free laborers, but the fact that they were *forced* to work and severely punished when they refused, constituted them slaves in reality. The royal recommendations to treat them well, to pay them for their work, and to teach them the Christian doctrines, were ignored by the masters, whose only object was to grow rich. The Indians were tasked far beyond their strength. They were ill-fed, often not fed at all, brutally ill-treated, horribly punished for trying to escape from the hellish yoke, ruthlessly slaughtered at the slightest show of resistance, so that thousands of them perished miserably. This had been the fate of the natives of la Española, and there can be no doubt that the Boriqueños had learned from fugitives of that island what was in store for them when Ponce ordered their distribution among the settlers.

The following list of Indians distributed in obedience to orders from the metropolis is taken from the work by Don Salvador Brau.[14] It was these first distributions, made in 1509-'10, which led to the rebellion of the Indians and the distributions that followed:

Indians

To the general treasurer, Pasamonte, a man described by Acosta as malevolent, insolent, deceitful, and sordid...... 300

To Juan Ponce de Leon.................................... 200

To Christopher Soto Mayor[15]...........................100

To Vicente Yañez Pinzón, on condition that he should settle in the island... 100

To Lope de Conchillos, King Ferdinand's Chief Secretary, as bad a character as Pasamonte.......................... 100

To Pedro Moreno and Jerome of Brussels, the delegate and clerk of Conchillos in Boriquén, 100 each..................200

To the bachelor-at-law Villalobos......................... 80

To Francisco Alvarado..................................... 80

A total of 1,060 defenseless Indians delivered into the ruthless hands of men steeped in greed, ambition, and selfishness.

FOOTNOTES:

[Footnote 10: The scanty remains of the first settlement were to be seen till lately in the Pueblo Viejo Ward, municipal district of Bayamón, along the road which loads from Cataño to Gurabó.]

[Footnote 11: He may have been the tenth or the twentieth if what the chroniclers tell us about the adoption of the defunct caciquess' names by their successors be true.]

[Footnote 12: The manioc of which the "casaba" bread is made.]

[Footnote 13: A "cascabel" (a measure the size of one of the round bells used in Spain to hang round the neck of the leader in a troop of mules) full of gold

17

and twenty-five pounds (an arroba) of cotton every three months for every Indian above sixteen years of age.]

[Footnote 14: Puerto Rico y su historia, p. 173.]

[Footnote 15: Among the Indians given to Soto Mayor was the sister of the cacique Guaybána second. She became his concubine, and in return for the preference shown her she gave the young nobleman timely warning of the impending rebellion.]

CHAPTER V
THE REBELLION
1511

The sullen but passive resistance of the Indians was little noticed by the Spaniards, who despised them too much to show any apprehension; but the number of fugitives to the mountains and across the sea increased day by day, and it soon became known that nocturnal "areytos" were held, in which the means of shaking off the odious yoke were discussed. Soto Mayor was warned by his paramour, and it is probable that some of the other settlers received advice through the same channels; still, they neglected even the ordinary precautions.

At last, a soldier named Juan Gonzalez, who had learned the native language in la Española, took upon himself to discover what truth there was in these persistent reports, and, naked and painted so as to appear like one of the Indians, he assisted at one of the nocturnal meetings, where he learned that a serious insurrection was indeed brewing; he informed Soto Mayor of what he had heard and seen, and the latter now became convinced of the seriousness of the danger.

Before Gonzalez learned what was going on, Guaybána had summoned the neighboring caciques to a midnight "areyto" and laid his plan before them, which consisted in each of them, on a preconcerted day, falling upon the Spaniards living in or near their respective villages; the attack, on the same day, on Soto Mayor's settlement, he reserved for himself and Guariónez, the cacique of Utuáo.

But some of the caciques doubted the feasibility of the plan. Had not the fugitives from Quisqueiá[16] told of the terrible effects of the shining blades they wore by their sides when wielded in battle by the brawny arms of the dreaded strangers? Did not their own arrows glance harmlessly from the glittering scales with which they covered their bodies? Was Guaybána quite sure that the white-faced invader could be killed at all? The majority thought that before undertaking their extermination they ought to be sure that they had to do with a mortal enemy.

Oviedo and Herrera both relate how they proceeded to discover this. Urayoán, the cacique of Yagüeca, was charged with the experiment. Chance soon favored him. A young man named Salcedo passed through his village to join some friends. He was hospitably received, well fed, and a number of men[17] were told to accompany him and carry his luggage. He arrived at the Guaorába, a river on the west side of the island, which flows into the bay of San German. They offered to carry him across. The youth accepted, was taken up between two of the strongest Indians, who, arriving in the middle of the river, dumped him under water—then they fell on him and held him down till he struggled no more. Dragging him

18

ashore, they now begged his pardon, saying that they had stumbled, and called upon him to rise and continue the voyage; but the young man did not move, he was dead, and they had the proof that the supposed demi-gods were mortals after all.

The news spread like wildfire, and from that day the Indians were in open rebellion and began to take the offensive, shooting their arrows and otherwise molesting every Spaniard they happened to meet alone or off his guard.

The following episode related by Oviedo illustrates the mental disposition of the natives of Boriquén at this period.

Aymamón, the cacique whose village was on the river Culebrinas, near the settlement of Soto Mayor, had surprised a lad of sixteen years wandering alone in the forest. The cacique carried him off, tied him to a post in his hut and proposed to his men a game of ball, the winner to have the privilege of convincing himself and the others of the mortality of their enemies by killing the lad in any way he pleased. Fortunately for the intended victim, one of the Indians knew the youth's father, one Pedro Juarez, in the neighboring settlement, and ran to tell him of the danger that menaced his son. Captain Diego Salazar, who in Soto Mayor's absence was in command of the settlement, on hearing of the case, took his sword and buckler and guided by the friendly Indian, reached the village while the game for the boy's life was going on. He first cut the lad's bonds, and with the words "Do as you see me do!" rushed upon the crowd of about 300 Indians and laid about him right and left with such effect that they had no chance even of defending themselves. Many were killed and wounded. Among the latter was Aymamón himself, and Salazar returned in triumph with the boy.

But now comes the curious part of the story, which shows the character of the Boriquén Indian in a more favorable light.

Aymamón, feeling himself mortally wounded, sent a messenger to Salazar, begging him to come to his caney or hut to make friends with him before he died. None but a man of Salazar's intrepid character would have thought of accepting such an invitation; but *he* did, and, saying to young Juarez, who begged his deliverer not to go: "They shall not think that I'm afraid of them," he went, shook hands with the dying chief, changed names with him, and returned unharmed amid the applauding shouts of "Salazar! Salazar!" from the multitude, among whom his Toledo blade had made such havoc. It was evident from this that they held courage, such as the captain had displayed, in high esteem. To the other Spaniards they used to say: "We are not afraid of *you*, for you are not Salazar."

* * * * *

It was in the beginning of June, 1511. The day fixed by Guaybána for the general rising had arrived. Soto Mayor was still in his grange in the territory under the cacique's authority, but having received the confirmation of the approaching danger from Gonzalez, he now resolved at once to place himself at the head of his men in the Aguáda settlement. The distance was great, and he had to traverse a country thickly peopled by Indians whom he now knew to be in open rebellion; but he was a Spanish hidalgo and did not hesitate a moment. The morning after receiving the report of Gonzalez he left his grange with that individual and four

19

other companions.

Guaybána, hearing of Soto Mayor's departure, started in pursuit. Gonzalez, who had lagged behind, was first overtaken, disarmed, wounded with his own sword, and left for dead. Near the river Yauco the Indians came upon Soto Mayor and his companions, and though there were no witnesses to chronicle what happened, we may safely assert that they sold their lives dear, till the last of them fell under the clubs of the infuriated savages.

That same night Guárionex with 3,000 Indians stealthily surrounded the settlement and set fire to it, slaughtering all who, in trying to escape, fell into their hands.[18]

In the interior nearly a hundred Spaniards were killed during the night. Gonzalez, though left for dead, had been able to make his way through the forest to the royal grange, situated where now Toa-Caja is. He was in a pitiful plight, and fell in a swoon when he crossed the threshold of the house. Being restored to consciousness, he related to the Spaniards present what was going on near the Culebrinas, and they sent a messenger to Capárra at once.

Immediately on receipt of the news from the grange, Ponce sent Captain Miguel del Toro with 40 men to the assistance of Soto Mayor, but he found the settlement in ashes and only the bodies of those who had perished.

FOOTNOTES:

[Footnote 16: La Española.]

[Footnote 17: The chroniclers say fifteen or twenty, which seems an exaggerated number.]

[Footnote 18: Salazar was able in the dark and the confusion of the attack on the settlement to rally a handful of followers, with whom he cut his way through the Indians and through the jungle to Capárra.]

CHAPTER VI

THE REBELLION *(continued)*

1511

Salazar's arrival at Capárra with a handful of wounded and exhausted men revealed to Ponce the danger of his situation. Ponce knew that it was necessary to strike a bold blow, and although, including the maimed and wounded, he had but 120 men at his disposal, he prepared at once to take the offensive.

Sending a messenger to la Española with the news of the insurrection and a demand for reenforcements, which, seeing his strained relations with the Admiral, there was small chance of his obtaining, he proceeded to divide his force in four companies of 30 men to each, and gave command to Miguel del Toro, the future founder of San German, to Louis de Añasco, who later gave his name to a province, to Louis Almanza and to Diego Salazar, whose company was made up exclusively of the maimed and wounded, and therefore called in good-humored jest the company of cripples.

Having learned from his scouts that Guaybána was camped with 5,000 to 6,000 men near the mouth of the river Coayúco in the territory between the Yauco and Jacágua rivers, somewhere in the neighborhood of the city which now bears the conqueror's name, he marched with great precaution through forest and jungle till he reached the river. He crossed it during the night and fell upon the Indians with such impetus that they believed their slain enemies to have come to life. They fled in confusion, leaving 200 dead upon the field.

The force under Ponce's command was too small to follow up his victory by the persecution of the terror-stricken natives; nor would the exhausted condition of the men have permitted it, so he wisely determined to return to Capárra, cure his wounded soldiers, and await the result of his message to la Española.

Oviedo and Navarro, whose narratives of these events are repeated by Abbad, state that the Boriquén Indians, despairing of being able to vanquish the Spaniards, called the Caribs of the neighboring islands to their aid; that the latter arrived in groups to make common cause with them, and that some time after the battle of Coayúco, between Caribs and Boriqueños, 11,000 men had congregated in the Aymacó district.

But Mr. Brau[19] calls attention to the improbability of such a gathering. "Guaybána," he says, "had been able, after long preparation, to bring together between 5,000 and 6,000 warriors—of these 200 had been slain, and an equal number, perhaps, wounded and made prisoners, so that, to make up the number of 11,000, at least as many Caribs as the entire warrior force of Boriquén must have come to the island in the short space of time elapsed since the first battle. The islands inhabited by the Caribs—Santa Cruz, San Eustaquio, San Cristobal, and Dominica—were too distant to furnish so large a contingent in so short a time, and the author we are quoting justly remarks that, admitting that such a feat was possible, they must have had at their disposition a fleet of at least 200 canoes, each capable of holding 20 men, a number which it is not likely they ever possessed."

There is another reason for discrediting the assertions of the old chroniclers in this respect. The idea of calling upon their enemies, the Caribs, to make common cause with them against a foe from whom the Caribs themselves had, as yet, suffered comparatively little, and the ready acceptance by these savages of the proposal, presupposes an amount of foresight and calculation, of diplomatic tact, so to speak, in both the Boriqueños and Caribs with which it is difficult to credit them.

The probable explanation of the alleged arrival of Caribs is that some of the fugitive Indians who had found a refuge in the small islands close to Boriquén may have been informed of the preparations for a revolt and of the result of the experiment with Salcedo, and they naturally came to take part in the struggle.

On hearing of the ominous gathering Ponce sent Louis Añasco and Miguel del Toro with 50 men to reconnoiter and watch the Indians closely, while he himself followed with the rest of his small force to be present where and when it might be necessary. Their approach was soon discovered, and, as if eager for battle, one cacique named Mabodomáca, who had a band of 600 picked men, sent the governor an insolent challenge to come on. Salazar with his company of cripples was chosen to silence him. After reconnoitering the cacique's position, he gave his men a much-needed rest till after midnight, and then dashed among them with his accustomed recklessness. The Indians, though taken by surprise, defended themselves bravely for three hours, "but," says Father Abbad, "God fought on the side of the Spaniards," and the result was that 150 dead natives were left on the field, with many wounded and prisoners. The Spaniards had not lost a man, though the majority had received fresh wounds.

Ponce, with his reserve force, arrived soon after the battle and found Salazar and his men resting. From them he learned that the main body of the Indians, to the number of several thousand, was in the territory of Yacüeca (now Añasco) and seemingly determined upon the extermination of the Spaniards.

The captain resolved to go and meet the enemy without regard to numbers. With Salazar's men and the 50 under Añasco and Toro he marched upon them at once. Choosing an advantageous position, he gave orders to form an entrenched camp with fascines as well, and as quickly as the men could, while he kept the Indians at bay with his arquebusiers and crossbowmen each time they made a rush, which they did repeatedly. In this manner they succeeded in entrenching themselves fairly well. The crossbowmen and arquebusiers went out from time to time, delivered a volley among the close masses of Indians and then withdrew. These tactics were continued during the night and all the next day, much to the disgust of the soldiers, who, wounded, weary, and hungry, without hope of rescue, heard the yells of the savages challenging them to come out of their camp. They preferred to rush among them, as they had so often done before. But Ponce would not permit it.

Among the arquebusiers the best shot was a certain Juan de Leon. This man had received instructions from Ponce to watch closely the movements of Guaybána, who was easily distinguishable from the rest by the "guanin," or disk of gold which he wore round the neck. On the second day, the cacique was seen to come and go actively from group to group, evidently animating his men for a general assault. While thus engaged he came within the range of Leon's arquebus, and a moment after he fell pierced by a well-directed ball. The effect was what Ponce had doubtless expected. The Indians yelled with dismay and ran far beyond the range of the deadly weapons; nor did they attempt to return or molest the Spaniards when Ponce led them that night from the camp and through the forest back to Capárra.

This was the beginning of the end. After the death of Guaybána no other cacique ever attempted an organized resistance, and the partial uprisings that took place for years afterward were easily suppressed. The report of the arquebus that laid Guaybána low was the death-knell of the whole Boriquén race.

The name of the island remained as a reminiscence only, and the island itself became definitely a dependency of the Spanish crown under the new name of San Juan Bautista de Puerto Rico.

FOOTNOTES:

[Footnote 19: Puerto Rico y su Historia, p. 189.]

22

CHAPTER VII
NUMBER OF ABORIGINAL INHABITANTS AND SECOND DISTRIBUTION OF INDIANS

1511-1515

Friar Bartolomé de Las Casas, in his Relation of the Indies, says with reference to this island, that when the Spaniards under the orders of Juan Ceron landed here in 1509, it was as full of people as a beehive is full of bees and as beautiful and fertile as an orchard. This simile and some probably incorrect data from the Geography of Bayaeete led Friar Iñigo Abbad to estimate the number of aboriginal inhabitants at the time of the discovery at 600,000, a number for which there is no warrant in any of the writings of the Spanish chroniclers, and which Acosto, Brau, and Stahl, the best authorities on matters of Puerto Rican history, reject as extremely exaggerated.

Mr. Brau gives some good reasons for reducing the number to about 16,000, though it seems to us that since little or nothing was known of the island, except that part of it in which the events related in the preceding chapters took place, any reasoning regarding the population of the whole island, based upon a knowledge of a part of it, is liable to error. Ponce's conquest was limited to the northern and western littoral; the interior with the southern and eastern districts were not settled by the Spaniards till some years after the death of Guaybána; and it seems likely that there were caciques in those parts who, by reason of the distance or other impediments, took no part in the uprising against the Spaniards. For the rest, Mr. Brau's reasonings in support of his reduction to 16,000 of the number of aborigines, are undoubtedly correct. They are: First. The improbability of a small island like this, *in an uncultivated state*, producing sufficient food for such large numbers. Second. The fact that at the first battle (that of Jacáguas), in which he supposes the whole available warrior force of the island to have taken part, there were 5,000 to 6,000 men only, which force would have been much stronger had the population been anything near the number given by Abbad; and, finally, the number of Indians distributed after the cessation of organized resistance was only 5,500, as certified by Sancho Velasquez, the judge appointed in 1515 to rectify the distributions made by Ceron and Moscoso, and by Captain Melarejo in his memorial drawn up in 1582 by order of the captain-general, which number would necessarily have been much larger if the total aboriginal population had been but 60,000, instead of 600,000.

* * * * *

The immediate consequence to the natives of the panic and partial submission that followed the death of their leader was another and more extensive distribution. The first distributions of Indians had been but the extension to San Juan of the system as practised in la Española, which consisted in granting to the crown officers in recompense for services or as an inducement to settle in the island, a certain number of natives.[20] In this way 1,060 Boriqueños had been disposed of in 1509 to 9 persons. The ill usage to which they saw them subjected drove the others to rebellion, and now, væ victis, the king, on hearing of the rebellion, wrote to Ceron and Diaz (July, 1511): "To 'pacify' the Indians you must

23

go well armed and terrorize them. Take their canoes from them, and if they refuse to be reduced with reason, make war upon them by fire and sword, taking care not to kill more than necessary, and send 40 or 50 of them to 'la Española' to serve us as slaves, etc." To Ponce he wrote on October 10th: "I give you credit for your labors in the 'pacification' and for having marked with an F on their foreheads all the Indians taken in war, making slaves of them and selling them to the highest bidders, separating the fifth part of the product for Us."

This time not only the 120 companions of Ponce came in for their share of the living spoils of war, but the followers of Ceron claimed and obtained theirs also.

The following is the list of Indians distributed after the battle of Yacüeca (if battle it may be called) as given by Mr. Brau, who obtained the details from the unpublished documents of Juan Bautista Muñoz:

Indians

To the estates (haciendas) of their royal Highnesses 500
Baltasar de Castro, the factor 200
Miguel Diaz, the chief constable 200
Juan Ceron, the mayor 150
Diego Morales, bachelor-at-law 150
Amador de Lares 150
Louis Soto Mayor 100
Miguel Diaz, Daux-factor 100
the (municipal) council 100
the hospitals 100
Bishop Manso 100
Sebastian de la Gama 90
Gil de Malpartida 70
Juan Bono (a merchant) 70
Juan Velasquez 70
Antonio Rivadeneyra 60
Gracian Cansino 60
Louis Aqueyo 60
the apothecary 60
Francisco Cereceda 50
40 other individuals 40 each 1,600

4,040
Distributed in 1509 1,060

Total 5,100

These numbers included women and children old enough to perform some kind of labor. They were employed in the mines, or in the rivers rather (for it was alluvium gold only that the island offered to the greed of the so-called conquerors); they were employed on the plantations as beasts of burden, and in every conceivable capacity under taskmasters who, in spite of Ferdinand's

24

revocation of the order to reduce them to slavery (September, 1514), had acted on his first dispositions and believed themselves to have the royal warrant to work them to death.

The king's more lenient dispositions came too late. They were powerless to check the abuses that were being committed under his own previous ordinances. The Indians disappeared with fearful rapidity. Licentiate Sancho Velasquez, who had made the second distribution, wrote to the king April 27, 1515: " ... Excepting your Highnesses' Indians and those of the crown officers, there are not 4,000 left." On August 8th of the same year the officers themselves wrote: " ... The last smeltings have produced little gold. Many Indians have died from disease caused by the hurricane as well as from want of food...."

To readjust the proportion of Indians according to the position or other claims of each individual, new distributions were resorted to. In these, some favored individuals obtained all they wanted at the expense of others, and as the number of distributable Indians grew less and less, reclamations, discontent, strife and rebellion broke out among the oppressors, who thus wreaked upon each other's heads the criminal treatment of the natives of which they were all alike guilty.

Such had been the course of events in la Española. The same causes had the same effects here. Herrera relates that when Miguel de Pasamente, the royal treasurer, arrived in the former island, in 1508, it contained 60,000 aboriginal inhabitants. Six years later, when a new distribution had become necessary, there were but 14,000 left—the others had been freed by the hand of death or were leading a wandering life in the mountains and forests of their island. In this island the process was not so rapid, but none the less effective.

FOOTNOTES:

[Footnote 20: The king's favorites in the metropolis, anxious to enrich themselves by these means, obtained grants of Indians and sent their stewards to administer them. Thus, in la Española, Conehillos, the secretary, had 1,100 Indians; Bishop Fonseca, 800; Hernando de la Vega, 200, and many others, "The Indians thus disposed of were, as a rule, the worst treated," says Las Casas.]

CHAPTER VIII
LAWS AND ORDINANCES
1511-1515

We have seen how Diego Columbus suspended Ponce in his functions as governor *ad interim*, and how the captain after obtaining from the king his appointment as permanent governor sent the Admiral's nominees prisoners to the metropolis. The king, though inclined to favor the captain, submitted the matter to his Indian council, which decided that the nomination of governors and mayors over the islands discovered by Christopher Columbus corresponded to his son. As a consequence, Ceron and Diaz were reinstated in their respective offices, and they were on their way back to San Juan a few months after Ponce's final success over the rebellious Indians.

Before their departure from Spain they received the following instructions, characteristic of the times and of the royal personage who imparted them:

"1. You will take over your offices very peaceably, endeavoring to gain the good-will of Ponce and his friends, that they may become *your* friends also, to the island's advantage.

"2. This done, you will attend to the 'pacification' of the Indians.

"3. Let many of them be employed in the mines and be well treated.

"4. Let many Indians be brought from the other islands and be well treated. Let the officers of justice be favored (in the distributions of Indians).

"5. Be very careful that no meat is eaten in Lent or other fast days, as has been done till now in la Española.

"6. Let those who have Indians occupy a third of their number in the mines.

"7. Let great care be exercised in the salt-pits, and one real be paid for each celemin[21] extracted, as is done in la Española.

"8. Send me a list of the number and class of Indians distributed, if Ponce has not done so already, and of those who have distinguished themselves in this rebellion.

"9. You are aware that ever since the sacraments have been administered in these islands, storms and earthquakes have ceased. Let a chapel be built at once with the advocation of Saint John the Baptist, and a monastery, though it be a small one, for Franciscan friars, whose doctrine is very salutary.

"10. Have great care in the mines and continually advise Pasamonte (the treasurer) or his agent of what happens or what may be necessary.

"11. Take the youngest Indians and teach them the Christian doctrine; they can afterward teach the others with better results.

"12. Let there be no swearing or blasphemy; impose heavy penalties thereon.

"13. Do not let the Indians be overloaded, but be well treated rather.

"14. Try to keep the Caribs from coming to the island, and report what measures it will be advisable to adopt against them. To make the natives do what is wanted, it will be convenient to take from them, with cunning (con maña), all the canoes they possess.

"15. You will obey the contents of these instructions until further orders.

Tordesillas, 25th of July, 1511.

F., King."

It is clear from the above instructions that, in the king's mind, there was no inconsistency in making the Indians work in the mines and their good treatment. There can be no doubt that both he and Doña Juana, his daughter, who, as heir to her mother, exercised the royal authority with him, sincerely desired the well-being of the natives as far as compatible with the exigencies of the treasury.

For the increase of the white population and the development of commerce and agriculture, liberal measures, according to the ideas of the age, were dictated as early as February, 1511, when the same commercial and political franchises were granted to San Juan as to la Española.

On July 25th the price of salt, the sale of which was a royal monopoly, was reduced by one-half, and in October of the same year the following rights and privileges were decreed by the king and published by the crown officers in Seville:

"1st. Any one may take provisions and merchandise to San Juan, which is now

26

being settled, and reside there with the same freedom as in la Española.

"2d. Any Spaniard may freely go to the Indies—that is, to la Española and to San Juan—by simply presenting himself to the officials in Seville, *without giving any further information* (about himself).

"3d. Any Spaniard may take to the Indies what arms he wishes, notwithstanding the prohibition.

"4th. His Highness abolishes the contribution by the owners of one 'castellano' for every Indian, they possess.

"5th. Those to whom the Admiral grants permission to bring Indians (from other islands) and who used to pay the fifth of their value (to the royal treasurer) shall be allowed to bring them free.

"6th. Indians once given to any person shall never be taken from him, except for delinquencies, punishable by forfeiture of property.

"7th. This disposition reduces the king's share in the produce of the gold-mines from one-fifth and one-ninth to one-fifth and one-tenth, and extends the privilege of working them from one to two years.

"8th. Whosoever wishes to conquer any part of the continent or of the gulf of pearls, may apply to the officials in Seville, who will give him a license, etc."

The construction of a smelting oven for the gold, of hospitals and churches for each new settlement, the making of roads and bridges and other dispositions, wise and good in themselves, were also decreed; but they became new causes of affliction for the Indians, inasmuch as *they* paid for them with their labor. For example: to the man who undertook to construct and maintain a hospital, 100 Indians were assigned. He hired them out to work in the mines or on the plantations, and with the sums thus received often covered more than the expense of maintaining the hospital.

The curious medley of religious zeal, philanthropy, and gold-hunger, communicated the first governors under the title of "instructions" did not long keep them in doubt as to which of the three—the observance of religious practises, the kind treatment of the natives, or the remittance of gold—was most essential to secure the king's favor. It was not secret that the monarch, in his *private* instructions, went straight to the point and wasted no words on religious or humanitarian considerations, the proof of which is his letter to Ponce, dated November 11, 1509. "I have seen your letter of August 16th. Be very diligent in searching for gold. Take out as much as you can, and having smolten it in la Española, send it at once. Settle the island as best you can. Write often and let Us know what happens and what may be necessary."

It was but natural, therefore, that the royal recommendations of clemency remained a dead letter, and that, under the pressure of the incessant demand for gold, the Indians were reduced to the most abject state of misery.

Until the year 1512 the Indians remained restless and subordinate, and in July, 1513, the efforts of the rulers in Spain to ameliorate their condition were embodied in what are known as the Ordinances of Valladolid.

These ordinances, after enjoining a general kind treatment of the natives, recommend that small pieces of land be assigned to them on which to cultivate corn, yucca, cotton, etc., and raise fowls for their own maintenance. The "encomendero," or master, was to construct four rustic huts for every 50 Indians. They were to be instructed in the doctrines of the Christian religion, the new-born babes were to be baptized, polygamy to be prohibited. They were to attend mass with their masters, who were to teach one young man in every forty to read. The boys who served as pages and domestic servants were to be taught by the friars in the convents, and afterward returned to the estates to teach the others. The men were not to carry excessively heavy loads. Pregnant women were not to work in the mines, nor was it permitted to beat them with sticks or whips under penalty of five gold pesos. They were to be provided with food, clothing, and a hammock. Their "areytos" (dances) were not to be interrupted, and inspectors were to be elected among the Spaniards to see that all these and former dispositions were complied with, and all negligence on the part of the masters severely punished.

The credit for these well-intentioned ordinances undoubtedly belongs to the Dominican friars, who from the earliest days of the conquest had nobly espoused the cause of the Indians and denounced the cruelties committed on them in no measured terms.

Friar Antonia Montesinos, in a sermon preached in la Española in 1511, which was attended by Diego Columbus, the crown officers, and all the notabilities, denounced their proceedings with regard to the Indians so vehemently that they left the church deeply offended, and that same day intimated to the bishop the necessity of recantation, else the Order should leave the island. The bishop answered that Montesinos had but expressed the opinion of the whole community; but that, to allay the scandal among the lower class of Spaniards in the island, the father would modify his accusations in the next sermon. When the day arrived the church was crowded, but instead of recantation, the intrepid monk launched out upon fresh animadversion, and ended by saying that he did so in the service not of God only, but of the king.

The officials were furious. Pasamonte, the treasurer, the most heartless destroyer of natives among all the king's officers, wrote, denouncing the Dominicans as rebels, and sent a Franciscan friar to Spain to support his accusation. The king was much offended, and when Montesinos and the prior of his convent arrived in Madrid to contradict Pasamonte's statements, they found the doors of the palace closed against them. Nothing daunted and imbued with the true apostolic spirit, they made their way, without asking permission, to the royal presence, and there advocated the cause of the Indians so eloquently that Ferdinand promised to have the matter investigated immediately. A council of theologians and jurists was appointed to study the matter and hear the evidence on both sides; but they were so long in coming to a decision that Montesinos and his prior lost patience and insisted on a resolution, whereupon they decided that the distributions were legal in virtue of the powers granted by the Holy See to the kings of Castilla, and that, if it was a matter of conscience at all, it was one for the king and his councilors, and not for the officials, who simply obeyed orders. The two Dominicans were ordered to return to la Española, and by the example of their virtues and mansuetude stimulate those who might be inclined to act wickedly.

The royal conscience was not satisfied, however, with the sophistry of his councilors, and as a quietus to it, the *well-meaning* ordinances just cited were enacted. They, too, remained a dead letter, and not even the scathing and persevering denunciations of Las Casas, who continued the good work begun by Montesinos, could obtain any practical improvement in the lot of the Indians until it was too late, and thousands of them had been crushed under the heel of the conqueror.

* * * * *

King Ferdinand's efforts to make Puerto Rico a prosperous colony were rendered futile by the dissensions between the Admiral's and his own partizans and the passions awakened by the favoritism displayed in the distribution of Indians. That the king took a great interest in the colonization of the island is shown by the many ordinances and decrees issued all tending to that end. He gave special licenses to people in Spain and in Santo Domingo to establish themselves in Puerto Rico.[22] In his minute instructions to Ponce and his successors he regulated every branch of the administration, and wrote to Ceron and Diaz: " ...I wish this island well governed and peopled as a special affair of mine." On a single day (February 26, 1511) he made, among others of a purely private character, the following public dispositions: "That the tithes and 'primicias'" [23] should be paid in kind only; that the fifth part of the output of the mines should be paid only during the first ten years; that he ceded to the colony for the term of four years all fines imposed by the courts, to be employed in the construction of roads and bridges; that the traffic between San Juan and la Española should be free, and that this island should enjoy the same rights and privileges as the other; that no children or grandchildren of people executed or burned for crimes or heresy should be admitted into the colony, and that an exact account should be sent to him of all the colonists, caciques, and Indians and their distribution.

He occupied himself with the island's affairs with equal interest up to the time of his death, in 1516. He made it a bishopric in 1512. In 1513 he disposed that the colonists were to build houses of adobe, that is, of sun-dried bricks; that all married men should send for their wives, and that useful trees should be planted. In 1514 he prohibited labor contracts, or the purchase or transfer of slaves or Indians "encomendados" (distributed). Finally, in 1515, he provided for the defense of the island against the incursions of the Caribs.

If these measures did not produce the desired result, it was due to the discord among the colonists, created by the system of "repartimientos" introduced in an evil hour by Columbus, a system which was the poisoned source of most of the evils that have afflicted the Antilles.

FOOTNOTES:

[Footnote 21: The twelfth part of a "fanega," equal to about two gallons, dry measure.]

[Footnote 22: Cedulas de vecindad.]

[Footnote 23: First-fruits.]

CHAPTER IX
THE RETURN OF CERON AND DIAZ—PONCE'S FIRST EXPEDITION TO FLORIDA
1511-1515

Ceron and Diaz returned to San Juan in November, 1511.

Before their departure from Seville they received sundry marks of royal favor. Among these was permission to Diaz and his wife to wear silken garments, and to transfer to San Juan the 40 Indians they possessed in la Española.

We have seen that the first article of the king's instructions to them enjoins the maintenance of friendly relations with Ponce, and in the distribution of Indians to favor those who had distinguished themselves in the suppression of the revolt.

They did nothing of the kind.

Their first proceeding was to show their resentment at the summary treatment they had received at the captain's hands by depriving him of the administration of the royal granges, the profits of which he shared with King Ferdinand, because, as his Highness explained to Pasamente in June, 1511, "Ponce received no salary as captain of the island."

They next sent a lengthy exposition to Madrid, accusing the captain of maladministration of the royal domain, and, to judge by the tenor of the king's letter to Ponce, dated in Burgos on the 23d of February, 1512, they succeeded in influencing him to some extent against his favorite, though not enough to deprive him of the royal patronage. "I am surprised," wrote the king, "at the small number of Indians and the small quantity of gold from our mines. The fiscal will audit your accounts, that you may be at liberty for the expedition to Bemini, which some one else has already proposed to me; but I prefer *you*, as I wish to recompense your services and because I believe that you will serve us better there than in our grange in San Juan, *in which you have proceeded with some negligence.*"

In the redistribution of Indians which followed, Ceron and Diaz ignored the orders of the sovereign and openly favored their own followers to the neglect of the conquerors', whose claims were prior, and whose wounds and scars certainly entitled them to consideration. This caused such a storm of protest and complaint against the doings of his protégés that Diego Columbus was forced to suspend them and appoint Commander Moscoso in their place.

This personage only made matters worse. The first thing *he* did was to practise another redistribution of Indians. This exasperated everybody to such an extent that the Admiral found it necessary to come to San Juan himself. He came, accompanied by a numerous suite of aspirants to different positions, among them Christopher Mendoza, the successor of Moscoso (1514). After the restoration of Ceron and Diaz in their offices, Ponce quietly retired to his residence in Capárra. He was wealthy and could afford to bide his time, but the spirit of unrest in him chafed under this forced inaction. The idea of discovering the island, said to exist somewhere in the northwestern part of these Indies, where wonderful waters flowed that restored old age to youth and kept youth always young, occupied his mind more and more persistently, until, having obtained the king's sanction, he fitted out an expedition of three ships and sailed from the port of Aguáda March

3, 1512.

Strange as it may seem, that men like Ponce, Zuñiga, and the other leading expeditionists should be glad of an opportunity to risk their lives and fortunes in the pursuit of a chimera, it must be remembered that the island of Bemini itself was not a chimera.

The followers of Columbus, the majority of them ignorant and credulous, had seen a mysterious new world rise, as it were, from the depths of the ocean. As the islands, one after the other, appeared before their astonished eyes, they discovered real marvels each day. The air, the land, the sea, were full of them. The natives pointed in different directions and spoke of other islands, and the adventurers' imaginations peopled them with fancied wonders. There was, according to an old legend, a fountain of perennial youth somewhere in the world, and where was it more likely to be found than in this hitherto unknown part of it?

Ponce and his companions believed in its existence as firmly as, some years later, Ferdinand Pizarro believed in the existence of El Dorado and the golden lake of Parimé.

The expedition touched at Guanakáni on the 14th of March, and on the 27th discovered what Ponce believed to be the island of which he was in search. On April 2d Ponce landed and took possession in the king's name. The native name of the island was Cansio or Cautix, but the captain named it "la Florida," some say because he found it covered with the flowers of spring; others, because he had discovered it on Resurrection day, called "Pascua Florida" by the Spanish Catholics.

The land was inhabited by a branch of the warlike Seminole Indians, who disputed the Spaniards' advance into the interior. No traces of gold were found, nor did the invaders feel themselves rejuvenated, when, after a wearisome march or fierce fight with the natives, they bathed in, or drank of, the waters of some stream or spring. They had come to a decidedly inhospitable shore, and Ponce, after exploring the eastern and southern littoral, and discovering the Cayos group of small islands, turned back to San Juan, where he arrived in the beginning of October, "looking much older," says the chronicler, "than when he went in search of rejuvenation."

Two years later he sailed for the Peninsula and anchored in Bayona in April, 1514. King Ferdinand received him graciously and conferred on him the titles of Adelantado of Bemini and la Florida, with civil and criminal jurisdiction on land and sea. He also made him commander of the fleet for the destruction of the Caribs, and perpetual "regidor" (prefect) of San Juan Bautista *de Puerto Rico*. This last surname for the island began to be used in official documents about this time (October, 1514).

The fleet for the destruction of the Caribs consisted of three caravels. With these, Ponce sailed from Bétis on May 14, 1515,[24] and reached the Leeward Islands in due course. In Guadeloupe, one of the Carib strongholds, he landed a number of men without due precaution. They were attacked by the natives. Fifteen of them were wounded, four of whom died. Some women who had been sent ashore to wash the soiled linen were carried off. Ponce's report of the event was laconic: "I wrote from San Lucas and from la Palma," he writes to the king (August 7th to 8th). "In Guadeloupe, while taking in water the Indians wounded some of my men. They shall be chastised." Haro, one of the crown officers in San Juan, informed the king afterward of all the circumstances of the affair, and added: "He (Ponce) left the (wounded) men in a deserted island on this side, which is Santa Cruz, and now he sends a captain, instead of going himself ..."

Ponce's third landing occurred June 15, 1515. He found the island in a deplorable condition. Discontent and disorder were rampant. The king had deprived Diego Columbus of the right to distribute Indians (January 23, 1513), and had commissioned Pasamonte to make a new distribution in San Juan. The treasurer had delegated the task to licentiate Sancho Velasquez, who received at the same time power to audit the accounts of all the crown officers. The redistribution was practised in September, 1514, with no better result than the former ones. It was impossible to satisfy the demands of all. The discontented were mostly Ponce's old companions, who overwhelmed the king with protests, while Velasquez defended himself, accusing Ponce and his friends of turbulence and exaggerated ambition.

As a consequence of all this strife and discord, the Indians were turned over from one master to another, distributed like cattle over different parts of the islands, and at each change their lot became worse.

Still, there were large numbers of them that had never yet been subjugated. Some, like the caciques of Humacáo and Daguáo, who occupied the eastern and southeastern parts of the island, had agreed to live on a peace footing with the Spaniards, but Ponce's impolitic proceeding in taking by force ten men from the village of the first-named chief caused him and his neighbor of Daguáo to burn their villages and take to the mountains in revolt. Many other natives had found a comparatively safe refuge in the islands along the coast, and added largely to the precarious situation by pouncing on the Spanish settlements along the coast when least expected. Governor Mendoza undertook a punitive expedition to Vieques, in which the cacique Yaureibó was killed; but the Indians had lost that superstitious dread of the Spaniards and of their weapons that had made them submit at first, and they continued their incursions, impeding the island's progress for more than a century.

FOOTNOTES:

[Footnote 24: Washington Irving says January.]

CHAPTER X
DISSENSIONS—TRANSFER OF THE CAPITAL
1515-1520

The total number of Spaniards in the island at the time of the rebellion did not exceed 200. Of these, between 80 and 100 were killed by the Indians. The survivors were reenforced, first by the followers of Ceron and Diaz, then by some stray adventurers who accompanied Diego Columbus on his visit to the island. We may assume, therefore, with Mr. Acosta,[25] that at the time of which we write the Spanish population numbered about 400, who Arángo, in a memorial addressed to the Cardinal Regent, classifies as Government officials, old conquerors, new hirelings, and "marrános hijos de reconciliados," which, translated, means, "vile brood of pardoned criminals," the latter being, in all probability, the immigrants into whose antecedents the king had recommended his officers in Seville not to inquire.

This population was divided into different hostile parties. The most powerful at the time was Ponce's party, led by Sedeño, the auditor, and Villafranca, the treasurer; opposed to whom were the partizans of Ceron and Diaz, the protégés of the Admiral, and those who had found favor with Velasquez, all of them deadly enemies because of the unequal division among them of the unhappy Indians.

The expedition to Florida and the honors conferred upon him by the king naturally enhanced Ponce's prestige among his old companions. Diego Columbus himself was fain to recognize the superior claim of him who now presented himself with the title Adelantado of Bemini and Florida, so that the captain's return to office was effected without opposition.

With his appointment as perpetual prefect, Ponce assumed the right to make a redistribution of Indians, but could not exercise it, because Sancho Velasquez had made one, as delegate of Pasamonte, only the year before (September, 1515).

In virtue of his special appointment as judge auditor of the accounts of all the crown officers, he had condemned Ponce during his absence to pay 1,352 gold pesos for shortcomings in his administration of the royal estates.[26]

The licentiate's report to the king, dated April 27, 1515, gives an idea of the state of affairs in San Juan at the time. " ... I found the island under tyranny, as will be seen from the documents I enclose. Juan Ceron and Miguel Diaz are responsible for 100,000 Castellanos[27] for Indians taken from persons who held them by schedule from your Highness."

"It would be well to send some bad characters away from here and some of the Admiral's creatures, on whom the rest count for protection."

"The treasurer (Haro) and the auditor are honest men. The accountant (Sedeño) is not a man to look after your Highness's interests. The place of factor is vacant."

"To your Highness 200 Indians have been assigned in Puerto Rico and 300 in San German."

A few days later (May 1, 1515) Velasquez himself was accused of gross abuse in the discharge of his duties by Iñigo de Zuñiga, who wrote to the king: " ... This licentiate has committed many injustices and offenses, as the attorney can testify. He gave Indians to many officers and merchants, depriving conquerors and settlers of them. He gambled much and always won, because they let him win in order to have him in good humor at the time of distribution of Indians. He carried away much money, especially from the 'Naborias.'" [28]

"He took the principal cacique, who lived nearest to the mines, for himself, and rented him out on condition that he keep sixteen men continually at work in the mines, and if any failed he was to receive half a ducat per head a day."

"He has taken Indians from other settlers and made them wash gold for himself, etc."

33

Before Ponce's departure for Spain the island had been divided into two departments or jurisdictions, the northern, with Capárra as its capital, under the direct authority of the governor, the southern division, with San German as the capital, under a lieutenant-governor, the chain of mountains in the interior being the mutual boundary. This division was maintained till 1782.

Capárra, or Puerto Rico, as it was now called, and San German were the only settlements when Ponce returned. The year before (1514) another settlement had been made in Daguáo, but it had been destroyed by the Caribs, and this ever-present danger kept all immigration away.

The king recognized the fact, and to obviate this serious difficulty in the way of the island's settlement, he wrote to his officers in Seville:

" ... Spread reports about the great quantities of gold to be found in Puerto Rico, and do not trouble about the antecedents of those who wish to go, for if not useful as laborers they will do to fight."

That Ferdinand was well aware of the insecurity of his hold on the island is shown by his subsequent dispositions. To the royal contractors or commissaries he wrote in 1514: "While two forts are being constructed, one in Puerto Rico and the other in San German, where, in case of rebellion, our treasure will be secure, you will give arms and ammunition to Ponce de Leon for our account, with an artilleryman, that he may have them in his house, which is to do duty as a fortress." And on May 14, 1515, he wrote from Medina del Campo: " ... Deliver to Ponce six 'espingardas.'" [29]

During this same period the island was constituted a bishopric, with Alonzo Manso, ex-sacristan of Prince John and cánon of Salamanca as prelate. He came in the beginning of 1513, when the intestine troubles were at their worst, bringing instructions to demand payment of tithes *in specie* and a royal grant of 150 Indians to himself, which, added to the fact that his presence would be a check upon the prevalent immorality, raised such a storm of opposition and intrigue against him that he could not exercise his functions. There was no church fit for services. This furnished him with a pretext to return to the Peninsula. When Ponce arrived the bishop was on the point of departure. There can be no doubt that King Ferdinand, in reappointing Ponce to the government of the island, trusted to the captain's military qualities for the reestablishment of order and the suppression of the attacks of the Caribs, but the result did not correspond to his Majesty's expectations.

Haro, the treasurer, reported to the king on October 6, 1515: " ... From the moment of his arrival Ponce has fomented discord. In order to remain here himself, he sent Zuñiga, his lieutenant, with the fleet. He caused the caciques Humacáo and Daguáo, who had but just submitted, to revolt again by forcibly taking ten men for the fleet."

The crown officers confirmed this statement in a separate report.

These accusations continued to the time of Ferdinand's death (February 23, 1516), when Cardinal Jimenez de Cisneros became Regent of Spain. This renowned prelate, whom Prince Charles, afterward Emperor Charles V, when confirming him in the regency, addressed as "the Very

Reverend Father in Christ, Cardinal of Spain, Archbishop of Toledo, Primate of all the Spanish Territories, Chief Chancellor of Castilla, our very dear and much beloved friend and master," was also Grand Inquisitor, and was armed with the tremendous power of the terrible Holy Office.

It was dangerous for the accusers and the accused alike to annoy such a personage with tales inspired by petty rivalries from an insignificant island in the West Indies. Nevertheless, one of the first communications from Puerto Rico that was laid before him was a memorial written by one Arángo, accusing Velasquez, among other things, of having given Indians to soldiers and to common people, instead of to conquerors and married men. "In Lent," says the accuser, "he goes to a grange, where he remains without hearing mass on Sundays, eating meat, and saying things against the faith ..."

The immediate effect of these complaints and mutual accusations was the suspension in his functions of Diego Columbus and the appointment of a triumvirate of Jerome friars to govern these islands. This was followed two years later by the return of Bishop Manso to San Juan, armed with the dreadful powers of General Inquisitor of the Indies and by the nomination of licentiate Antonio de la Gama as judge auditor of the accounts of Sancho Velasquez. The judge found him guilty of partiality and other offenses, and on June 12, 1520, wrote to the regent: "I have not sent the accounts of Sancho Velasquez, because it was necessary that he should go with them, but the bishop of this island has taken him for the Holy Inquisition *and he has died in prison*."

The Jerome fathers on their way to la Española, in 1516, touched at what they describe as "the port of Puerto Rico, which is in the island of San Juan de Boriquén," and the treasurer, Haro, wrote of them on January 21, 1518: " ... They have done nothing during the year, and the inhabitants are uncertain and fear changes. This is the principal cause of harm to the Indians. It is necessary to dispose what is to be done ... Although great care is now exercised in the treatment of the Indians their numbers grow less for all that, because just as they are ignorant of things concerning the faith, so do they ignore things concerning their health, and they are of very weak constitution."

The frequent changes in the government that had been made by Diego Columbus, the arrest of Velasquez and his death in the gloomy dungeons of the Inquisition, the arrival of de la Gama as judge auditor and governor *ad interim*, and his subsequent marriage with Ponce's daughter Isabel, all these events but served to embitter the strife of parties. "The spirit of vengeance, ambition, and other passions had become so violent and deep-rooted among the Spaniards," says Abbad,[30] "that God ordained their chastisement in various ways."

The removal of the capital from its swampy location to the islet which it now occupies was another source of dissension. It appears that the plan was started immediately after Ceron's accession, for the king wrote to him November 9, 1511: "Juan Ponce says that he located the town in the best part of the island. We fear that you want to change it. You shall not do so without our special order. If there is just reason for change you must inform us first."

35

Velasquez, in his report of April, 1515, mentions that he accompanied the Town Council of Capárra to see the site for the new capital, and that to him it seemed convenient.

In 1519 licentiate Rodrigo de Figueroa sent a lengthy exposition accompanied by the certified declarations of the leading inhabitants regarding the salubrity of the islet and the insalubrity of Capárra, with a copy of the disposition of the Jerome fathers authorizing the transfer, and leaving Ponce, who strenuously opposed it, at liberty to live in his fortified house in Capárra as long as he liked.

On November 16, 1520, Baltazar Castro, in the name of the crown officers of San Juan, reported to the emperor: "The City of Puerto Rico has been transferred to an islet which is in the port where the ships anchor, a very good and healthy location."

FOOTNOTES:

[Footnote 25: Annotations, p. 96.]

[Footnote 26: Ponce protested and appealed to the Audiencia, but did not obtain restitution till 1520.]

[Footnote 27: A Castellano was the 150 part of a mark of gold. The mark had 8 ounces.]

[Footnote 28: Indians distributed to be employed as domestic servants.]

[Footnote 29: Small pieces of ordnance.]

[Footnote 30: XII, p. 89.]

CHAPTER XI
CALAMITIES—PONCE'S SECOND EXPEDITION TO FLORIDA AND DEATH

1520-1537

Among the calamities referred to by Friar Abbad as visitations of Providence was one which the Spaniards had brought upon themselves. Another epidemic raged principally among the Indians. In January, 1519, the Jerome friars wrote to the Government from la Española: " ... It has pleased our Lord to send a pestilence of smallpox among the Indians here, and nearly one-third of them have died. We are told that in the island of San Juan the Indians have begun to die of the same disease."

Another scourge came in the form of ants. "These insects," says Abbad, quoting from Herrera, "destroyed the yucca or casabe, of which the natives made their bread, and killed the most robust trees by eating into their roots, so that they turned black, and became so infected that the birds would not alight on them. The fields were left barren and waste as if fire from heaven had descended on them. These insects invaded the houses and tormented the inmates night and day. Their bite caused acute pains to adults and endangered the lives of children. The affliction was general," says Abbad, "but God heard the people's vows and the pests disappeared." The means by which this happy result was obtained are described by Father Torres Vargas: "Lots were drawn to see what saint should be chosen as the people's advocate before God. Saint Saturnine was returned, and the plague ceased at once."

"Some time after there appeared a worm which also destroyed the yucca. Lots were again drawn, and this time Saint Patrick came out; but the bishop and the ecclesiastical chapter were of opinion that this saint, being little venerated, had no great influence in heaven. Therefore, lots were drawn again and again, three times, and each time the rejected saint's name came out. This was clearly a miracle, and Saint Patrick was chosen as advocate. To atone for their unwillingness to accept him, the chapter voted the saint an annual mass, sermon, and procession, which was kept up for many years without ever anything happening again to the casabe ..."

To the above-described visitations, nature added others and more cruel ones. These were the destructive tempests, called by the Indians Ouracan.

The first hurricane since the discovery of the island by Columbus of which there is any record happened in July, 1515, when the crown officers reported to the king that a great storm had caused the death of many Indians by sickness and starvation. On October 4, 1526, there was another, which Juan de Vadillo described thus: " ... There was a great storm of wind and rain which lasted twenty-four hours and destroyed the greater part of the town, with the church. The damage caused by the flooding of the plantations is greater than any one can estimate. Many rich men have grown poor, among them Pedro Moreno, the lieutenant-governor."

In July and August, 1530, the scourge was repeated three times in six weeks, and Governor Lando wrote to Luis Columbus, then Governor of la Española: " ... The storms have destroyed all the plantations, drowned many cattle, and caused a great dearth of food. Half of the houses in this city have been blown down; of the other half those that are least damaged are without roofs. In the country and at the mines not a house is left standing. Everybody has been impoverished and thinking of going away. There are no more Indians and the land must be cultivated with negroes, who are a monopoly, and can not be brought here for less than 60 or 70 'castellanos' apiece. The city prays that the payment of all debts may be postponed for three years."

Seven years later (1537), three hurricanes in two months again completely devastated the island. " ... They are the greatest that have been experienced here," wrote the city officers. " ... The floods have carried away all the plantations along the borders of the rivers, many slaves and cattle have been drowned, want and poverty are universal. Those who wanted to leave the island before are now more than ever anxious to do so."

The incursions of Caribs from the neighboring islands made the existence of the colony still more precarious. Wherever a new settlement was made, they descended, killing the Spaniards, destroying the plantations, and carrying off the natives.

* * * * *

The first news of the wonderful achievements of Cortez in Mexico reached San Juan in 1520, and stirred the old adventurer Ponce to renewed action. On February 10, 1521, he wrote to the emperor: "I discovered Florida and some other small islands at my own expense, and now I am going to settle them with plenty of men and two ships, and I am going to explore the coast, to see if it compares with the lands (Cuba) discovered by Velasquez. I will leave here in four or five days, and beg your Majesty to favor me, so that I may be enabled to carry out this great enterprise."

Accordingly, he left the port of Aguáda on the 26th of the same month with two ships, well provided with all that was necessary for conquest.

But the captain's star of fortune was waning. He had a stormy passage, and when he and his men landed they met with such fierce resistance from the natives that after several encounters and the loss of many men, Ponce himself being seriously wounded, they were forced to reembark. Feeling that his end was approaching, the captain did not return to San Juan, but sought a refuge in Puerto Principe, where he died.

One of his ships found its way to Vera Cruz, where its stores of arms and ammunition came as a welcome accession to those of Cortez.

The emperor bestowed the father's title of Adelantado of Florida and Bemini on his son, and the remains of the intrepid adventurer, who had found death where he had hoped to find perennial youth, rested in Cuban soil till his grandchildren had them transferred to this island and buried in the Dominican convent.

A statue was erected to his memory in 1882. It stands in the plaza of San José in the capital and was cast from the brass cannon left behind by the English after the siege of 1797.

CHAPTER XII
INCURSIONS OF FUGITIVE BORIQUÉN INDIANS AND CARIBS
1530-1582

The conquest of Boriquén was far from being completed with the death of Guaybána.

The panic which the fall of a chief always produces among savages prevented, for the moment, all organized resistance on the part of Guaybána's followers, but *they* did not constitute the whole population of the island. Their submission gave the Spaniards the dominion over that part of it watered by the Culebrinas and the Añasco, and over the northeastern district in which Ponce had laid the foundations of his first settlement. The inhabitants of the southern and eastern parts of the island, with those of the adjacent smaller islands, were still unsubdued and remained so for years to come. Their caciques were probably as well informed of the character of the newcomers and of their doings in la Española as was the first Guaybána's mother, and they wisely kept aloof so long as their territories were not invaded.

The reduced number of Spaniards facilitated the maintenance of a comparative independence by these as yet unconquered Indians, at the same time that it facilitated the flight of those who, having bent their necks to the yoke, found it unbearably heavy. According to "Regidor" (Prefect) Hernando de Mogollon's letter to the Jerome fathers, fully one-third of the "pacified" Indians—that is, of those who had submitted—had disappeared and found a refuge with their kinsmen in the neighboring islands.

The first fugitives from Boriquén naturally did not go beyond the islands in the immediate vicinity. Vieques, Culébras, and la Mona became the places of rendezvous whence they started on their retaliatory expeditions, while their spies or their relatives on the main island kept them informed of what was passing. Hence, no sooner was a new settlement formed on the borders or in the neighborhood of some river than they pounced upon it, generally at night, dealing death and destruction wherever they went.

In vain did Juan Gil, with Ponce's two sons-in-law and a number of tried men, make repeated punitive expeditions to the islands. The attacks seemed to grow bolder, and not till Governor Mendoza himself led an expedition to Vieques, in which the cacique Yaureibó was killed, did the Indians move southeastward to Santa Cruz.

That the Caribs[31] inhabiting the islands Guadeloupe and Dominica made common cause with the fugitives from Boriquén is not to be doubted. The Spaniard was the common enemy and the opportunity for plunder was too good to be lost. But the primary cause of all the so-called Carib invasions of Puerto Rico was the thirst for revenge for the wrongs suffered, and long after those who had smarted under them or who had but witnessed them had passed away, the tradition of them was kept alive by the areytos and songs, in the same way as the memory of the outrages committed by the soldiers of Pizarro in Peru are kept alive *till this day* among the Indians of the eastern slope of the Andes. The fact that neither Jamaica nor other islands occupied by Spaniards were invaded, goes to prove that in the case of Puerto Rico the invasions were prompted by bitter resentment of natives who had preferred exile to slavery, coupled, perhaps, with a hope of being able to drive the enemies of their race from their island home, a hope which, if it existed, and if we consider the very limited number of Spaniards who occupied it, was not without foundation.

* * * * *

It was Nemesis, therefore, and not the mere lust of plunder, that guided the Boriquén Indians and their Carib allies on their invasions of Puerto Rico.

Diego Columbus during his visit in 1514 had founded a settlement with 50 colonists along the borders of the Daguáo and Macáo rivers on the eastern coast.

They had constructed houses and ranchos, introduced cattle, and commenced their plantations, but without taking any precautions against sudden attacks or providing themselves with extra means of defense.

One night they were awakened by the glare of fire and the yells of the savages. As they rushed out to seek safety they fell pierced with arrows or under the blows of the terrible Macánas. Very few of them escaped.

The next attack was in the locality now constituting the municipal district of Loiza.

This place was settled by several Spaniards, among them Juan Mexia, a man said to have been of herculean strength and great courage. The Indian woman with whom he cohabited had received timely warning of the intended attack, a proof that communications existed between the supposed Caribs and the Indians on the island. She endeavored to persuade the man to seek safety in flight, but he disdained to do so. Then she resolved to remain with him and share his fate. Both were killed, and Alejandro Tapia, a native poet, has immortalized the woman's devotion in a romantic, but purely imaginative, composition.

Ponce's virtual defeat in Guadeloupe made the Caribs bolder than ever. They came oftener and in larger numbers, always surprising the settlements that were least prepared to offer resistance. Five years had elapsed since the destruction of Daguáo. A new settlement had gradually sprung up in the neighborhood along the river Humacáo and was beginning to prosper, but it was also doomed. On November 16, 1520, Baltazar Castro, one of the crown officers, reported to the emperor:

"It is about two months since 5 canoes with 150 Carib warriors came to this island of San Juan and disembarked in the river Humacáo, near some Spanish settlements, where they killed 4 Christians and 13 Indians. From here they went to some gold mines and then to some others, killing 2 Christians at each place. They burned the houses and took a fishing smack, killing 4 more. They remained from fifteen to twenty days in the country, the Christians being unable to hurt them, having no ships. They killed 13 Christians in all, and as many Indian women, and '*carried off*' 50 natives. They will grow bolder for being allowed to depart without punishment. It would be well if the Seville officers sent two light-draft vessels to occupy the mouths of the rivers by which they enter."

On April 15, 1521, a large number of Indians made a descent on the south coast, but we have no details of their doings; and in 1529 their audacity culminated in an attempt on the capital itself. La Gama's report to the emperor of this event is as follows: "On the 18th of October, after midnight, 8 large pirogues full of Caribs entered the bay of Puerto Rico, and meeting a bark on her way to Bayamón, manned by 5 negroes and some other people, they took her. Finding that they had been discovered, they did not attempt a landing till sunrise, then they scuttled the bark. Some shots fired at them made them leave. Three negroes were found dead, pierced with arrows. The people of this town and all along the coast are watching. Such a thing as this has not been heard of since the discovery. A fort, arms, artillery, and 2 brigantines of 30 oars each, and no Caribs will dare to come. If not sent, fear will depopulate the island."

In the same month of the following year (1530) they returned, and this time landed and laid waste the country in the neighborhood of the capital. The report of the crown officers is dated the 31st of October: "Last Sunday, the 23d instant, 11 canoes, in which there may have been 500 Caribs, came to this island and landed at a point where there are some agricultural establishments belonging to people of this city. It is the place where the best gold in the island is found, called Daguáo and the mines of Llagüello. Here they plundered the estate of Christopher Guzman, the principal settler. They killed him and some other Christians,[32] whites, blacks, and Indians, besides some fierce dogs, and horses which stood ready saddled. They burned them all, together with the houses, and committed many cruelties with the Christians. They carried off 25 negroes and Indians, *to eat them, as is their wont*. We fear that they will attack the defenseless city in greater force, and the fear is so great that the women and children dare not sleep in their houses, but go to the church and the monastery, which are built of stone. We men guard the city and the roads, being unable to attend to our business.

"We insist that 2 brigantines be armed and equipped, as was ordered by the Catholic king. No Caribs will then dare to come. Let the port be fortified or the island will be deserted. The governor and the officers know how great is the need, but they may make no outlays without express orders."

As a result of the repeated requests for light-draft vessels, 2 brigantines were constructed in Seville in 1531 and shipped, in sections, on board of a ship belonging to Master Juan de Leon, who arrived in June, 1532. The crown officers immediately invited all who wished to man the brigantines and make war on the Caribs, offering them as pay half of the product of the sale of the slaves they should make, the other half to be applied to the purchase of provisions.

The brigantines were unfit for service. In February, 1534, the emperor was informed: "Of the brigantines which your Majesty sent for the defense of this island only the timber came, and half of that was unfit.... We have built brigantines with the money intended for fortifications."

Governor Lando wrote about the same time: "We suffer a thousand injuries from the Caribs of Guadeloupe and Dominica. They come every year to assault us. Although the city is so poor, we have spent 4,000 pesos in fitting out an expedition of 130 men against them; but, however much they are punished, the evil will not disappear till your Majesty orders these islands to be settled." The expedition referred to sailed under the orders of Joan de Ayucar, and reached Dominica in May, 1534. Fifteen or 16 villages of about 20 houses each were burned, 103 natives were killed, and 70 prisoners were taken, the majority women and boys. The Spaniards penetrated a distance of ten leagues into the interior of the island, meeting with little resistance, because the warrior population was absent. Eight or 10 pirogues and more than 20 canoes were also burned. With this punishment the fears of the people in San Juan were considerably allayed.

In 1536 Sedeño led an expedition against the Caribs of Trinidad and Bartholomé. Carreño fitted out another in 1539. He brought a number of slaves for sale, and the crown officers asked permission to brand them on the forehead, "as is done in la Española and in Cubágua."

The Indians returned assault for assault. Between the years 1564 and 1570 they were specially active along the southern coast of San Juan, so that Governor Francisco Bahamonde Lugo had to take the field against them in person and was wounded in the encounter. Loiza, which had been resettled, was destroyed for the second time in 1582, and a year or so later the Caribs made a night attack on Aguáda, where they destroyed the Franciscan convent and killed 3 monks.

With the end of the sixteenth and the commencement of the seventeenth centuries the West Indian archipelago became the theater of French and English maritime enterprise. The Carib strongholds were occupied, and by degrees their fierce spirit was subdued, their war dances relinquished, their war canoes destroyed, their traditions forgotten, and the bold savages, once the terror of the

41

West Indian seas, succumbed in their turn to the inexorable law of the survival of the fittest.

FOOTNOTES:

[Footnote 31: The West Indian islands were inhabited at the time of discovery by at least three races of different origin. One of these races occupied the Bahamas. Columbus describes them as simple, peaceful creatures, whose only weapon was a pointed stick or cane. They were of a light copper color, rather good-looking, and probably had formerly occupied the whole eastern part of the archipelago, whence they had been driven or exterminated by the Caribs, Caribós, or Guáribos, a savage, warlike, and cruel race, who had invaded the West Indies from the continent, by way of the Orinoco. The larger Antilles, Cuba, la Española, and Puerto Rico, were occupied by a race which probably originated from some southern division of the northern continent. The chroniclers mention the Guaycures and others as their ancestors, and Stahl traces their origin to a mixture of the Phoenicians with the Aborigines of remote antiquity]

[Footnote 32: Abbad says 30.]

CHAPTER XIII
DEPOPULATION OF THE ISLAND—PREVENTIVE MEASURES—INTRODUCTION OF NEGRO SLAVES
1515-1534

The natural consequence of natural calamities and invasions was the rapid disappearance of the natives. "The Indians are few and serve badly," wrote Sedeño in 1515, about the same time that the crown officers, to explain the diminution in the gold product, wrote that many Indians had died of hunger, as a result of the hurricane. " … The people in la Mona," they said, "have provided 310 loads of bread, with which we have bought an estate in San German. It will not do to bring the Indians of that island away, because they are needed for the production of bread."

Strenuous efforts to prevent the extinction of the Indians were made by Father Bartolomé Las Casas, soon after the death of King Ferdinand. This worthy Dominican friar had come to the court for the sole purpose of denouncing the system of "encomiendas" and the cruel treatment of the natives to which it gave rise. He found willing listeners in Cardinal Cisneros and Dean Adrian, of Lovaino, the regents, who recompensed his zeal with the title of "Protector of the Indians." The appointment of a triumvirate of Jerome friars to govern la Española and San Juan (1517) was also due to Las Casas's efforts. Two years later the triumvirate reported to the emperor that in compliance with his orders they had taken away the Indians from all non-resident Spaniards in la Española and had collected them in villages.

Soon after the emperor's arrival in Spain Las Casas obtained further concessions in favor of the Indians. Not the least important among these were granted in the schedule of July 12, 1520, which recognized the principle that the Indians were born free, and contained the following dispositions:

1st. That in future no more distributions of Indians should take place.

2d. That all Indians assigned to non-residents, from the monarch downward, should be *ipse facto* free, and be established in villages, under the authority of their respective caciques; and

3d. That all residents in these islands, who still possessed Indians, were bound to conform strictly, in their treatment of them, to the ordinances for their protection previously promulgated.

Antonio de la Gama was charged with the execution of this decree. He sent a list of non-residents, February 15,1521, with the number of Indians taken from each, his Majesty himself heading the list with 80. The total number thus liberated was 664.

These dispositions created fierce opposition. Licentiate Figueroa addressed the emperor on the subject, saying: " ... It is necessary to overlook the 'encomiendas,' otherwise the people will be unable to maintain themselves, and the island will be abandoned."

However, the crown officers ascribe the licentiate's protest to other motives than the desire for the good of the island. "He has done much harm," they wrote. "He has brought some covetous young men with him and made them inspectors. They imposed heavy fines and gave the confiscated Indians to their friends and relations. He and they are rich, while the old residents have scarcely wherewith to maintain themselves."

But Figueroa had foreseen these accusations, for he concludes his above-mentioned letter to the emperor, saying: " ... Let your Majesty give no credence to those who complain. Most of them are very cruel with the Indians, and care not if they be exterminated, provided they themselves can amass gold and return to Castilla."

Martin Fernandez Enciso, a bachelor-at-law, addressed to the emperor a learned dissertation intended to refute the doctrine that the Indians were born free, maintaining that the right of conquest of the New World granted by the Pope necessarily included the right to reduce the inhabitants to slavery.

And thus, in spite of the philanthropic efforts of Las Casas, of the well-intentioned ordinances of the Catholic kings, and of the more radical measures sanctioned by Charles V, the Indian's lot was not bettered till it was too late to save him from extinction.

"The Indians are dying out!" This is the melancholy refrain of all the official communications from 1530 to 1536. The emperor made a last effort to save the remnant in 1538, and decreed that all those who still had Indians in their possession should construct stone or adobe houses for them under penalty of losing them. In 1543 it was ordained by an Order in Council that all Indians still alive in Cuba, la Española, and Puerto Rico, were as free as the Spaniards themselves, and they should be permitted to loiter and be idle, "that they might increase and multiply."

Bishop Rodrigo Bastidas, who was charged to see to the execution of this order in Puerto Rico, still found 80 Indians to liberate. Notwithstanding these terminant orders, so powerless were they to abolish the abuses resulting from the iniquitous system, that as late as 1550 the Indians were still treated as slaves. In that year

Governor Vallejo wrote to the emperor: "I found great irregularity in the treatment of these few Indians, ... they were being secretly sold as slaves, etc."

Finally, in 1582, Presbyter Ponce de Leon and Bachelor-at-Law Santa Clara, in a communication to the authorities, stated: "At the time when this island was taken there were found here and distributed 5,500 Indians, without counting those who would not submit, and to-day there is not one left, excepting 12 or 15, who have been brought from the continent. They died of disease, sarampion, rheum, smallpox, and ill-usage, or escaped to other islands with the Caribs. The few that remain are scattered here and there among the Spaniards on their little plantations. Some serve as soldiers. They do not speak their language, because they are mostly born in the island, and they are good Christians." This is the last we read of the Boriquén Indians.

* * * * *

With the gradual extinction of the natives, not only the gold output ceased, but the cultivation of ginger, cotton, cacao, indigo, etc., in which articles a small trade had sprung up, was abandoned. The Carib incursions and hurricanes did the rest, and the island soon became a vast jungle which everybody who could abandoned.

"We have been writing these last four years," wrote the crown officers, February 26, 1534, "that the island is becoming depopulated, the gold is diminishing, the Indians are gone. Some new gold deposits were discovered in 1532, and as much as 20,000 pesos were extracted. We thought this would contribute to the repeopling of the island, but the contrary has happened. The people, ruined by the hurricanes of the year 1530, thinking that they might find other gold deposits, bought negroes on credit at very high prices to search for them. They found none, and have not been able to pay their creditors. Some are fugitive in the mountains, others in prison, others again have stolen vessels belonging to the Administration and have gone with their negroes no one knows where. With all this and the news from Peru, not a soul would remain if they were not stopped."

When the news of the fabulous riches discovered in Peru reached this island, the desire to emigrate became irresistible. Governor Lando wrote to the emperor, February 27, 1534: " ... Two months ago there came a ship here from Peru to buy horses. The captain related such wonderful things that the people here and in San German became excited, and even the oldest settlers wanted to leave. If I had not instantly ordered him away the island would have been deserted. *I have imposed the death penalty on whosoever shall attempt to leave the island.*"

On July 2d he wrote again: " ... Many, mad with the news from Peru, have secretly embarked in one or other of the numerous small ports at a distance from the city. Among the remaining settlers even the oldest is constantly saying: 'God help me to go to Peru.' I am watching day and night to prevent their escape, but can not assure you that I shall be able to retain the people.

"Two months ago I heard that some of them had obtained possession of a ship at a point on the coast two leagues from here and intended to leave. I sent three vessels down the coast and twenty horsemen by land. They resisted, and my presence was required to take them. Three were killed and others wounded. *I ordered some of them to be flogged and cut off the feet of others*, and then I had to

44

dissimulate the seditious cries of others who were in league with them and intended to join them in la Mona, which is twelve leagues from here. If your Majesty does not promptly remedy this evil, I fear that the island will be entirely depopulated or remain like a country inn. This island is the key and the entrance to all the Antilles. The French and English freebooters land here first. The Caribs carry off our neighbors and friends before our very eyes. If a ship were to come here at night with fifty men, they could burn the city and kill every soul of us. I ask protection for this noble island, now so depopulated that one sees scarcely any Spaniards, only negroes …"

But even the negro population was scarce. The introduction of African slaves into la Española had proceeded *pari passu* with the gradual disappearance of the Indians. As early as 1502 a certain Juan Sanchez had obtained permission to introduce five caravels of negro slaves into that island free of duty, though Ovando complained that many of them escaped to the mountains and made the Indians more insubordinate than ever; but in San Juan a special permission to introduce negroes was necessary. Geron in 1510 and Sedeño in 1512 were permitted to bring in two negroes each only by swearing that they were for their own personal service. In 1513 the general introduction of African slaves was authorized by royal schedule, but two ducats per head had to be paid for the privilege. Cardinal Cisneros suspended the export of slaves from Spain in 1516, but the emperor sanctioned it again in 1517, to stop, if possible, the destruction of the natives.

Father Las Casas favored the introduction of African slaves for the same reason, and obtained from the emperor a concession in favor of his high steward, Garrebod, to send 4,000 negroes to la Española, Cuba, and Puerto Rico. Garrebod sold the concession to a Genovese firm (1517), but negroes remained very scarce and dear in San Juan till 1530, when, by special dispensation of the empress in favor of some merchants, 200 negroes were brought to this island. They were greedily taken up on credit at exorbitant prices, which caused the ruin of the purchasers and made the city authorities of San Juan petition her Majesty April 18, 1533, praying that no more negro ¡slaves might be permitted to come to the island for a period of eighteen months, because of the inability of the people to pay for them.

In Governor Lando's letter of July, 1534, above quoted, he informs the emperor that in the only two towns that existed in the island at that time (San Juan and San German) there were "very few Spaniards and only 6 negroes in each." The incursions of the French and English freebooters, to which he refers in the same letter, had commenced six years before, and these incursions bring the tale of the island's calamities to a climax.

45

CHAPTER XIV
ATTACKS BY FRENCH PRIVATEERS—CAUSE OF THE WAR WITH FRANCE—CHARLES V.—RUIN OF THE ISLAND
1520-1556

The depredations committed by the privateers, which about this time began to infest the Antilles and prey upon the Spanish possessions, were a result of the wars with almost every nation in Europe, in which Spain became involved after the accession of Charles, the son of Juana, daughter of Ferdinand and Isabella and Philip I, Archduke of Austria.

The young prince had been educated amid all the pomp and splendor of the imperial court. He was a perfect type of the medieval cavalier, who could break a lance with the proudest knight in the empire, and was worthy in every respect of the high destiny that awaited him. At the age of twenty he became the heir to eight kingdoms,[33] the recognized ruler of the Netherlands, lord of vast territories in Africa, and absolute arbiter of the destinies of the Spanish division of the New World.

Scarcely had this powerful young prince been accepted and crowned by the last and most recalcitrant of his kingdoms (Cataluña), and while still in Barcelona, the news arrived of the death of his grandfather, Maximilian, King of the Romans and Emperor elect of Germany. Intrigues for the possession of the coveted crown were set on foot at once by the prince, now Charles I of Spain and by Francis I, King of France. The powers ranged themselves on either side as their interests dictated. Henry VIII of England declared himself neutral; Pope León X, who distrusted both claimants, was waiting to see which of them would buy his support by the largest concessions to the temporal power of the Vatican; the Swiss Cantons hated France and sided with Charles; Venice favored Francis I.[34]

The German Diet assembled at Frankfort June 17, 1519, and unanimously elected Frederick of Saxony, surnamed the Prudent. He showed his prudence by declining the honor, and in an address to the assembly dwelt at some length on the respective merits of the two pretenders, and ended by declaring himself in favor of the Spanish prince, one reason for his preference being that Charles was more directly interested in checking the advance of the Turks, who, under Soleiman the Magnificent, threatened, at the time, to overrun the whole of eastern Europe.

Charles I of Spain was elected, and thus became Charles V, King of the Romans and Emperor of Germany—that is, the most powerful monarch of his time, before he had reached the age of manhood. His success, added to other political differences and ambitions, was not long in provoking a war with France, which, with short intervals, lasted the lifetime of the two princes.

* * * * *

Spain was most vulnerable in her ultramarine possessions. They offered tempting prizes to the unscrupulous, adventurous spirits of the period, and the merchants on the coast of Normandy asked and obtained permission to equip privateers to harass Spanish commerce and attack the unprotected settlements.

San Juan was one of the first to suffer. An official report dated September 26,

1528, informs us that "on the day of the Apostle Saint John a French caravel and a tender bore down on the port of Cubágua and attempted to land artillery from the ship with the help of Indians brought from Margarita, five leagues distant. On the 12th of August they took the town of San German, plundered and burned it; they also destroyed two caravels that were there...."

French privateers were sighted off the coast continually, but it would seem that the island, with its reputation for poverty, its two settlements 40 leagues apart, and scanty population, offered too little chance for booty, so that no other landing is recorded till 1538, when a privateer was seen chasing a caravel on her way to San German. The caravel ran ashore at a point two leagues from the capital and the crew escaped into the woods. The Frenchmen looted the vessel and then proceeded to Guadianilla, where they landed 80 men, 50 of them arquebusiers. They burned the town, robbed the church and Dominican convent; but the people, after placing their families in security, returned, and under favor of a shower of rain, which made the arquebuses useless, fell upon them, killed 15 and took 3 prisoners, in exchange for whom the stolen church property was restored. The people had only 1 killed.

The attack was duly reported to the sovereign, who ordered the construction of a fort, and appointed Juan de Castellanos, the treasurer, its commander (October 7, 1540). The treasurer's reply is characteristic: "The fort which I have been ordered to make in the town of San German, of which I am to be the commander, shall be made as well as we may, though there is great want of money ... and of carts, negroes, etc. It will be necessary to send masons from Sevilla, as there is only 1 here, also tools and 20 negroes....

"Forts for this island are well enough, but it would be better to favor the population, lending money or ceding the revenues for a few years, to construct sugar-mills...."

On June 12th of the same year the treasurer wrote again announcing that work on the San German fort had commenced, for which purpose he had bought some negroes and hired others at *two and a half pesos per month.*

But on February 12, 1542, the crown officers, including Castellanos, reported that *the emperor's order to suspend work on the fort of San German had been obeyed.*

In February, 1543, the bishop wrote to the emperor: "The people of San German, for fear of the French privateers, have taken their families and property into the woods. If there were a fort they would not be so timid nor would the place be so depopulated."

As late as September, 1548, he reported: "I came here from la Española in the beginning of the year to visit my diocese. I disembarked in San German with an order from the Audiencia to convoke the inhabitants, and found that there were a few over 30, who lived half a league from the port for fear of the privateers. They don't abandon the important place, but there ought to be a fort."

But the prelate pleaded in vain.

Charles V, occupied in opposing the French king's five armies, could not be expected to give much attention to the affairs of an insignificant island in a remote corner of his vast dominions. Puerto Rico was left to take care of itself, and San German's last hour struck on Palm Sunday, 1554, when 3 French ships entered the port of Guadianilla, landed a detachment of men who penetrated a league inland, plundering and destroying whatever they could. From that day San German, the settlement founded by Miguel del Toro in 1512, disappeared from the face of the land.

The capital remained. No doubt it owed its preservation from French attacks to the presence of a battery and some pieces of artillery which, as a result of reiterated petitions, had been provided. The population also was more numerous. In 1529 there were 120 houses, some of them of stone. The cathedral was completed, and a Dominican convent was in course of construction with 25 friars waiting to occupy it. Thus, one by one, all the original settlements disappeared. Guánica, Sotomayor, Daguáo, Loiza, had been swept away by the Indians. San German fell the victim of the Spanish monarch's war with his neighbor. The only remaining settlement, the capital, was soon to be on the point of being sacrificed in the same way. The existence of the island seemed to be half-forgotten, its connection with the metropolis half-severed, for the crown officers wrote in 1536 that *no ship from the Peninsula had entered its ports for two years.*

"Negroes and Indians," says Abbad, "seeing the small number of Spaniards and their misery, escaped to the mountains of Luquillo and Añasco, whence they descended only to rob their masters."

FOOTNOTES:

[Footnote 33: Castilla and Aragón, Navarro, Valencia, Cataluña, Mallorca, Sicily, and Naples.]

[Footnote 34: Hista. general de España por Don Modesto Lafuente. Barcelona, 1889.]

CHAPTER XV
SEDEÑO—CHANGES IN THE SYSTEM OF GOVERNMENT
1534-1555

A slight improvement in the gloomy situation of the people of San Juan took place when, driven by necessity, they began to dedicate themselves to agriculture. At this time, too (1535), Juan Castellanos, the island's attorney at the court, returned with his own family and 75 colonists. Yet scarcely had they had time to settle when they were invited to remigrate by one of Ponce's old companions.

This was Sedeño, a perfect type of the Spanish adventurer of the sixteenth century—restless, ambitious, unscrupulous. The king had made him "contador" (comptroller) of San Juan in 1512 and perpetual "regidor" (alderman) in 1515. In 1518 we find him in prison under accusation of having brought a woman and child from a convent in Sevilla. He broke out of the prison and escaped in a ship. In 1521 he was in prison again for debt to the Government. On this occasion the judge auditor wrote to the emperor: " ... It is said of the comptroller that he has put his hands deep into your Majesty's treasure. He is the one who causes most strife and unrest in the island, ... everybody says that it would be well if he were removed." In 1524 Villasante accused him of malversation of public funds. In 1531 he appears as Governor of Trinidad, accused of capturing natives of the neighboring continent, branding them and selling them as slaves. In 1532, reinstated in his post as comptroller, he leaves Alonzo de la Fuente as his deputy and goes on an expedition to conquer Trinidad. In 1535 he complains to the emperor that the authorities in San Juan have not assisted him in his enterprise, and in the following year the governor and crown officers address a complaint against him to the empress, saying: "Sedeño presented a schedule authorizing him to bring 200 men from the Canary Islands to make war with fire and sword on the Caribs of Trinidad, and permitting him, or any other person authorized by him, to fit out an expedition for the same purpose here.

"Under this pretext he has collected people to go to the conquest of Meta. We wrote to the Audiencia in la Española, and an order came that he should not go beyond the limits of his government, but he continues his preparations and has already 50 horses and 120 men on the continent, and is now going with some 200 men more and another 100 horses. He takes no notice of your Majesty's commands, collects people from all parts without a license, and causes grave injury to the island, because since the rage for going to Peru began the population is very scarce and we can not remedy the evil...."

This restless adventurer died of fever on the continent in 1538. Sedeño's emigration schemes deprived the island of many of its best settlers. The wish to abandon it was universal. Lando's drastic measures to prevent it roused the people's anger, and they clamored for his removal. The Audiencia sent Juan Blasquez as judge auditor, and Vasco de Tiedra was appointed Lando's successor in 1536. But in the following year a radical change was made in the system of government.

The quarrels, the jealousies, and mutual accusations between the colonists and the Government officials that kept the island in a continual ferment, were the natural consequence of the prerogatives exercised by Diego Columbus, which permitted him to fill all lucrative positions in the island with his own favorites, often without any regard to their aptitude.

The incessant communications to the emperor, and even to the empress, on every subject more or less connected with the public service, but dictated mostly by considerations of self-interest, coming, as they did, from the smallest and poorest and least important of his Majesty's possessions, must have been a source of great annoyance to the imperial ministers, consequently they resolved to remove the cause. The Admiral was deprived of the prerogative of appointing governors, and henceforth the alcaldes (mayors) and "chief alguaciles" (high constables), to be elected from among the colonists by a body of eight aldermen (regidores), were to exercise the governmental functions for one year at a time, and could not be reelected till two years after the first nomination. The wisdom of this innovation was not generally acknowledged. The crown officers wrote: " ... All are not agreed on the point whether the governor should or should not be elected among the residents of the island. For the country's good he should, no doubt, be a resident."

Alonzo la Fuente was of a different opinion. He wrote in November, 1536: "It has been a great boon to take the appointment of governors out of the Admiral's hands. As a rule, some neighbor or friend was made supreme judge, and he usually proceeded with but little regard for the island's welfare. All the rest were servants and employees of the Admiral, which caused me much uneasiness, seeing the results. Appoint a governor, but a man from abroad, not a resident." In the following year he wrote regarding the elective system just introduced: " ... If the alcaldes must take cognizance of everything, this will become a place of confusion and disorder. A few will lord it over all the rest, and the alcaldes themselves will but be their creatures."

The new system of government was unsatisfactory. Castro and Castellanos asked for the appointment of a supreme judge in March, 1539, because an appeal to the authorities in la Española was made against every decision of the alcalde. Alderman La Fuente and Martel confirmed this in December, 1541. They wrote: " ... There is great want of a supreme judge. More than fifteen homicides have been committed in less than eight years, and only one of the delinquents has been punished ..." In January, 1542, the city officers sent a deputy to lay their grievances before the emperor, not daring to write them "for their lives," and in February the island's attorney, Alonzo Molina, stated the causes of the failure of the elective system to be the ignorance of the laws of those in authority and the reduced number of electors. "It is necessary," he said, "to name a mayor or governor who is a man of education and conscience, *not a resident*, because the judges have their 'compadres.'[35] The governor must be a man of whom they stand in fear, and if some one of this class is not sent soon, he will find few to govern, for the majority intend to abandon the island."

A law passed, it appears, at the petition of a single individual, in 1542, increased the confusion and discord still more. This law made the pastures of the island, as well as the woods and waters, public property. The woods and waters had been considered such from the beginning, but the pastures, included in the concessions of lands made at different times by the crown, were private property. The result of this law was aggression on the part of the landless and resistance on the part of the proprietors, with the consequent scenes of violence and civil strife.

Representations against the law were made by the ecclesiastical chapter, by the city attorney, and by the three crown officers in February, 1542; but the regidores, on the other hand, insisted on the compliance with the royal mandate, and reported that when the law was promulgated, all the possessors of cattle-ranges opposed it, and four of their body who voted for compliance with the law were threatened to be stoned to death and have their eyes pulled out. "We asked to have the circumstance testified to by a notary, and it was refused. We wanted to write to your Majesty, and to prevent any one conveying our letters, they bought the whole cargo of the only ship in port, and did the same with another ship that came in afterward...."

On the 2d of June following they wrote again: " ... An alcalde, two aldermen, and ten or twelve wealthy cattle-owners wanted to kill us. We had to lock ourselves up in our houses.... The people here are so insubordinate that if your Majesty does not send some one to chastise them and protect his servants, there will soon be no island of San Juan."

50

The system of electing annual governors among the residents was abolished in 1544, and the crown resumed its prerogative with the appointment of Gerónimo Lebrón, of la Española, as governor for one year. He died fifteen days after his arrival, and the Audiencia named licentiate Cervantes de Loayza in his place, who was compelled to imprison some of the ringleaders in the party of opposition against the pasture laws. This governor wrote to the emperor in July, 1545: " ... I came to this island with my wife and children to serve your Majesty, but I found it a prey to incredible violences...."

Cervantes was well received at first, and the city officials asked the emperor to prorogue his term of office, but as Bishop Bastidas said of the islanders, it was not in their nature to be long satisfied with any governor, and the next year they clamored for his "residencia." He rendered his accounts and came out without blame or censure.

It appears that about the year 1549 the system of electing alcaldes as governors was resumed, for in that year Bishop Bastidas thanks the emperor, and tells him "the alcaldes were sufficient, considering the small population." But in 1550 we again find a governor appointed by the crown for five years, a Doctor Louis Vallejo, from whose communications describing the conditions of the island we extract the following: "It is a pity to see how the island has been ruined by the attacks of Frenchmen and Caribs. The few people that remain in San German live in the worst possible places, in swamps surrounded by rough mountains, a league from the port...." And on the 4th of December, 1550: " ... The island was in a languishing condition because the mines gave out, but now, with the sugar industry, it is comparatively prosperous. The people beg your Majesty's protection."

However, in October, 1553, we find Bishop Alonzo la Fuente and others addressing King Philip II, and telling him that "the land is in great distress, ... traffic has ceased for fear of the corsairs...." The same complaints continue during 1554 and 1555. Then Vallejo is subjected to "residencia" by the new governor, Estevéz, who, after a few months' office, is "residentiated" in his turn by Caráza, who had been governor in 1547.

After this the chronicles are so scanty that not even the diligent researches of Friar Abbad's commentator enabled him to give any reliable information regarding the government of the island. It remained the almost defenseless point of attack for the nations with which Spain was constantly at war, and this small but bright pearl in her colonial crown was preserved only by fortunate circumstances on the one hand and the loyalty of the inhabitants on the other.

FOOTNOTES:
[Footnote 35: Protectors or protégés—literally, "godfathers."]

CHAPTER XVI
DEFENSELESS CONDITION OF THE ISLAND— CONSTRUCTION OF FORTIFICATIONS AND CIRCUMVALLATION OF SAN JUAN

1555-1641

San German disappeared for want of means of defense, and if the French privateers of the time had been aware that the forts in San Juan were without guns or ammunition it is probable that this island would have become a French possession.

The defenses of the island were constructed by the home authorities in a very dilatory manner. Ponce's house in Capárra had been fortified in a way so ineffective that Las Casas said of it that the Indians might knock it down butting their heads against it. This so-called fort soon fell in ruins after the transfer of the capital to its present site. There is no information of what became of the six "espingardas" (small ordnance or hand-guns) with which it had been armed at King Ferdinand's expense. They had probably been transferred to San Juan, where, very likely, they did good service intimidating the Caribs.

In 1527 an English ship came prowling about San Juan bay, la Mona, and la Española, and this warning to the Spanish authorities was disregarded, notwithstanding Blas de Villasante's urgent request for artillery and ammunition.

After the burning of San German by a French privateer in August, 1537, Villasante bought five "lombardas" (another kind of small ordnance) for the defense of San Juan. In 1529 and 1530 both La Gama, the acting governor, and the city officers represented to the emperor the necessity of constructing fortifications, "*because the island's defenseless condition caused the people to emigrate.*"

It appears that the construction of the first fort commenced about 1533, for in that year the Audiencia in la Española disposed of some funds for the purpose, and Governor Lando suggested the following year that if the fort were made of stone "it would be eternal." The suggestion was acted upon and a tax levied on the people to defray the expense.

This fort must have been concluded about the year 1540, for in that same year the ecclesiastical and the city authorities were contending for the grant of the slaves, carts, and oxen that had been employed, the former wanting them for the construction of a church, the latter for making roads and bridges.

This "Fortaleza" is the same edifice which, after many changes, was at last, and is still, used as a gubernatorial residence, the latest reconstruction being effected in 1846.[36] As a fort, Gonzalez Fernandez de Oviedo denounced it as a piece of useless work which, "if it had been constructed by blind men could not have been located in a worse place," and in harmony with his advice a battery was constructed on the rocky promontory called "the Morro."

San Juan had now a fort (1540) but no guns. The crown officers, reporting an attack on Guayáma by a French privateer in 1541, again clamor for artillery. Treasurer Castellanos writes in March and June of the same year: "The artillery for this fort has not yet arrived. How are we to defend it?"

Treasurer Salinas writes in 1554: "The French have taken several ships. It would

52

have been a great boon if your Majesty had ordered Captain Mindirichága to come here with his four ships to defend this island and la Española. He would have found Frenchmen in la Mona, where they prepare for their expeditions and lay in wait. They declare their intention to take this island, and it will be difficult for us to defend it without artillery or other arms. If there is anything in the fort it is useless, nor is the fort itself of any account. It is merely a lodging-house. The bastion on the Morro, if well constructed, could defend the entrance to the harbor with 6 pieces. We have 60 horsemen here with lances and shields, but no arquebusiers or pikemen. Send us artillery and ammunition."

The demand for arms and ammunition continued in this way till 1555, when acting Governor Caráza reported that 8 pieces of bronze ordnance had been planted on the Morro.

The existing fortifications of San Juan have all been added and extended at different periods. Father Torres Vargas, in his chronicles of San Juan, says that the castle grounds of San Felipe del Morro were laid out in 1584. The construction cost 2,000,000 ducats.[37] The Boquerón, or Santiago fort, the fort of the Cañuelo, and the extensions of the Morro were constructed during the administration of Gabriel Royas (1599 to 1609). Governor Henriquez began the circumvallation of the city in 1630, and his successor, Sarmiento, concluded it between the years 1635 and 1641. Fort San Cristobal was begun in the eighteenth century and completed in 1771. Some fortifications of less importance were added in the nineteenth century.

When Caráza reported, in 1555, that the first steps in the fortification of the capital had been taken, the West Indian seas swarmed with French privateers, and their depredations on Spanish commerce and ill-protected possessions continued till Philip II signed the treaty of peace at Vervins in 1598.

But before that, war with England had been declared, and a more formidable enemy than the French was soon to appear before the capital of this much-afflicted island.

FOOTNOTES:

[Footnote 36: The inscription on the upper front wall of the building is: "During the reign of her Majesty, Doña Isabel II, the Count of Mirasol being Captain-General, Santos Cortijo, Colonel of Engineers, reconstructed this royal fort in 1846."]

[Footnote 37: Ducat, a coin struck by a duke, worth, in silver, about $1.15, in gold, twice as much. It was also a nominal money worth eleven pesetas and one maravedi.]

CHAPTER XVII
DRAKE'S ATTACK ON SAN JUAN
1595

Of all the English freebooters that preyed upon Spain and her colonies from the commencement of the war in 1585 to the signing of peace in 1604, Francis Drake was the greatest scourge and the most feared.

Drake early distinguished himself among the fraternity of sea-rovers by the boldness of his enterprises and the intensity of his hatred of the Spaniards. When still a young man, in 1567-'68, he was captain of a small ship, the Judith, one of a fleet of slavers running between the coast of Africa and the West Indies, under the command of John Hawkyns, another famous freebooter. In the harbor of San Juan de Ulúa the Spaniards took the fleet by stratagem; the Judith and the Minion, with Hawkyns on board, being the only vessels that escaped. Young Drake's experiences on that occasion fixed the character of his relations to the Dons forever afterward. He vowed that they should pay for all he had suffered and all he had lost.

At that time the Spaniards were ostensibly still friends with England. To Drake they were then and always treacherous and forsworn enemies. In 1570 he made a voyage to the West Indies in a bark of forty tons with a private crew. In the Chagres River, on the coast of Nombre de Dios, there happened to be sundry barks transporting velvets and taffetas to the value of 40,000 ducats, besides gold and silver. They were all taken.

Two years later he made a most daring attempt to take the town of Nombre de Dios, and would probably have succeeded had he not been wounded. He fainted from loss of blood. His men carried him back on board and suspended the attack. On his recovery he met with complete success, and returned to Plymouth in 1573 with a large amount of treasure openly torn from a nation with which England was at peace, arriving at the very time that Philip's ambassador to Queen Elizabeth was negotiating a treaty of peace. Drake had no letters of marque, and consequently was guilty of piracy in the eyes of the law, the penalty for which was hanging. The Spaniards were naturally very angry, and clamored for restitution or compensation and Drake's punishment, but the queen, who shared the pirate's hatred of the Spaniards, sent him timely advice to keep out of the way.

In 1580 he returned from another voyage in the West Indies, just when a body of so-called papal volunteers had landed in Ireland. They had been brought by a Spanish officer in Spanish ships, and the queen, pending a satisfactory explanation, refused to receive Mendoza, the Spanish ambassador, and hear his complaints of Drake's piracies. When his ships had been brought round in the Thames, she visited him on board and conferred on him the honor of knighthood. From this time onward he became a servant of the crown.[38]

It was this redoubtable sea-rover who, according to advices received early in 1595, was preparing an expedition in England for the purpose of wresting her West Indian possessions from Spain. The expedition was brought to naught, through the disagreements between Drake and Hawkyns, who both commanded it, by administrative blunders and vexatious delays in England. The Spaniards were everywhere forewarned and goaded to action by the terror of Drake's name.

Notwithstanding this, the island's fate, seeing its defenseless condition, would, no doubt, have been sealed at that time but for a most fortunate occurrence which brought to its shores the forces that enabled it to repulse the attack. Acosta's annotations on Abbad's history contains the following details of the events in San Juan at the time:

"General Sancho Pardo y Osorio sailed from Havana March 10, 1595, in the flagship of the Spanish West Indian fleet, to convoy some merchantmen and convey 2,000,000 pesos in gold and silver, the greater part the property of his Majesty the king. The flagship carried 300 men.

"On the 15th, when in the Bermuda channel, a storm separated the convoy from the other ships, sent her mainmast overboard, broke her rudder, and the ship sprang a leak. In this condition, after a consultation among the officers, it was decided to repair the damage as well as possible and steer for Puerto Rico, which they reached on the 9th of April. The treasure was placed in security in the fort and messengers despatched to the king to learn his Majesty's commands.

"A few days later official advice of the preparations in England was brought to the island in a despatch-boat. Governor Juarez, General Sancho, and the commander of the local infantry held a council, in which it was resolved to land the artillery from the dismasted ship and sink her and another vessel in the channel at the entrance to the harbor, while defenses should be constructed at every point where an enemy could attempt a landing. The plan was carried out under the direction of General Sancho, who had ample time, as no enemy appeared during the next seven months.

"On the 13th of November 5 Spanish frigates arrived under the command of Pedro Tello de Gúzman, with orders from the king to embark the treasure forthwith and take it to Spain; but Tello, on his way hither, had fallen in off Guadeloupe with two English small craft, had had a fight with one of them, sank it, and while pursuing the other had come suddenly in sight of the whole fleet, which made him turn about and make his way to Puerto Rico before the English should cut him off. From the prisoners taken from the sunken vessel he had learned that the English fleet consisted of 6 line-of-battle ships of 600 to 800 tons each, and about 20 others of different sizes, with launches for landing troops, 3,000 infantry, 1,500 mariners, all well armed and provided with artillery, bound direct for Puerto Rico under the command of Sir Francis Drake and John Hawkyns.

"Tello's 5 frigates made a very important addition to the island's defenses. Part of his men were distributed among the land forces, and his ships anchored in the bay, just behind the two sunken ships.

"All was now ready for a determined resistance. General Sancho had charge of the shore defenses, Admiral Gonzalo Mendez de Cauzo commanded the forts, Tello, with his frigates and 300 men, defended the harbor. The bishop promised to say a mass and preach a sermon every day, and placed a priest at every post to give spiritual aid where necessary. Lastly, despatch-boats were sent to la Española and to Cuba to inform the authorities there of the coming danger.

"The defensive forces consisted of 450 men distributed at different points on shore with 34 pieces of ordnance of small caliber. In the forts there were 36 pieces, mostly bronze ordnance, with the respective contingent of men. On board of Tello's frigates there were 300 men.

"General Sancho, after an inspection of the defenses, assured the governor that the island was safe if the men would but fight.

"At daybreak on the 22d of November the English fleet hove in sight. The call

55

to arms was sounded, and everybody," says the chronicler, "ran joyfully to his post."

A caravel with some launches showing white flags came on ahead, sounding, but on passing the Boquerón were saluted with a cannon shot, whereupon they withdrew replacing the white flags by red ones.

The whole fleet now came to anchor in front of the "Caleta del Cabron" (Goat's Creek), much to the surprise of the islanders, who had no idea that there was anchoring ground at that point; but, being within range of the 3 pieces of cannon on the Morrillo and of the 2 pieces planted at the mouth of the creek, they were fired upon, with the result, as became known afterward, of considerable damage to the flagship and the death of 2 or 3 persons, among them Hawkyns, Drake's second in command.

This unexpectedly warm reception made it clear to the English admiral that the islanders had been forewarned and were not so defenseless as they had been reported. Some launches were sent to take soundings in the vicinity of Goat Island, and at 5 in the afternoon the fleet lifted anchor and stood out to sea. Next morning at 8 o'clock it returned and took up a position under the shelter of the said island, out of range of the artillery on the forts.

More soundings were taken during the day in the direction of Bayamón, as far as the Cañuelo. That night, about 10 o'clock, 25 launches, each containing from 50 to 60 men, advanced under cover of the darkness and attacked Tello's frigates. The flames of 3 of the ships, which the English succeeded in firing, soon lit up the bay and enabled the artillery of the 3 forts to play with effect among the crowded launches. The Spaniards on board Tello's ships succeeded in putting out the fire on board 2 of the ships, the third one was destroyed. After an hour's hard fighting and the loss by the English, as estimated by the Spanish chronicler, of 8 or 10 launches and of about 400 men, they withdrew. The Spanish loss that night was 40 killed and some wounded.

The next day the English fleet stood out to sea again, keeping to windward of the harbor, which made Tello suspect that they intended to return under full sail when the wind sprang up and force their way into the harbor. To prevent this, 2 more ships and a frigate were sunk across the entrance with all they had on board, there being no time to unload them.

As expected, the fleet came down at 4 o'clock in the afternoon, but did not try to force an entrance. It quietly took up the same position between the Morro and Goat Island, which it had occupied the day before, and this made the Spaniards think that another night attack on the 3 remaining frigates was impending. After dark the frigates were removed to a place of safety within the bay.

The night passed without an alarm. The next day the English launches were busy all day sounding the bay as far as the Boquerón, taking care to keep out of range of the artillery on shore. Night came on and when next morning the sun lit up the western world there was not an enemy visible. Drake had found the island too well prepared and deemed it prudent to postpone the conquest.

Two days later news came from Arecibo that the English fleet had passed that port. A messenger sent to San German returned six days later with the information that the enemy had been there four days taking in wood and water and had sailed southward on the 9th of December.

It is said that when Drake afterward learned that his abandonment of the conquest of Puerto Rico had made him miss the chance of adding 2,000,000 pesos in gold and silver to the Maiden Queen's exchequer, he pulled his beard with vexation.

FOOTNOTES:

[Footnote 38: Drake and his Successors. The Edinburgh Review, July, 1901.]

CHAPTER XVIII
OCCUPATION AND EVACUATION OF SAN JUAN BY LORD GEORGE CUMBERLAND—CONDITION OF THE ISLAND AT THE END OF THE SIXTEENTH CENTURY

Puerto Rico and his Majesty's treasure were now safe. When there was no longer any fear of the enemy's return, haste was made to reembark the money and get rid of General Sancho and Tello and their men who were fast consuming the island's scanty resources.

Two years after Drake's ineffectual attack on the island another English fleet, with a large body of troops under the orders of Lord George Cumberland, came to Puerto Rico. A landing was effected at Cangrejos (the present Santurce). The bridge leading to the capital was not then fortified, but its passage was gallantly disputed by Governor Antonio Mosquera, an old soldier of the war in Flanders. The English were far superior in numbers and armament, and Mosquera had to fall back. Captain Serralta, the brothers John and Simon Sanabria, and other natives of the island, greatly distinguished themselves in this action. The English occupied the capital and the forts without much more opposition. An epidemic of dysentery and yellow fever carried off 400 Englishmen in less than three months and bid fair to exterminate the whole invading force, so that, to save his troops, the English commander was obliged to evacuate the island, which he did on the 23d of November. He carried with him 70 pieces of artillery of all sizes which he found in the fortifications. The city itself he left unhurt, except that he took the church-bells and organ and carried off an artistically sculptured marble window in one of the houses which had taken his fancy.

Mr. Brau mentions some documents in the Indian archives of Spain, from which it appears that another invasion of Puerto Rico took place a year after Cumberland's departure. On that occasion the governor and the garrison were carried off as prisoners, but as there was a cruel epidemic still raging in the island at the time the English did not stay.

The death of Philip II (September 13, 1598) and of his inveterate enemy, Queen Elizabeth (March 24, 1603), brought the war with England to a close. The ambassador of Philip III in London negotiated a treaty of peace with James I, which was signed and ratified in the early part of 1604.

So ended the sixteenth century in Boriquén. If the dictum of Las Casas, that the island at the century's beginning was "as populous as a beehive and as lovely as an orchard," was but a rhetorical figure, there is no gainsaying the fact that at the time of Ponce's landing it was thickly peopled, not only that part occupied by the Spaniards but *the whole island*, with a comparatively innocent, simple, and peaceably disposed native race. The end of the century saw them no more. The erstwhile garden was an extensive jungle. The island's history during these hundred years was condensed into the one word "strife." All that the efforts of the king and his governors had been able to make of it was a penal settlement, a presidio with a population of about 400 inhabitants, white, black, and mongrel. The littoral was an extensive hog-and cattle-ranch, with here and there a patch of sugar-cane; there was no commerce.[39] There were no roads. The people, morally, mentally, and materially poor, were steeped in ignorance and vice. Education there was none. The very few who aspired to know, went to la Española to obtain an education. The few spiritual wants of the people were supplied by monks, many of them as ignorant and bigoted as themselves. War and pestilence and tempest had united to wipe the island from the face of the earth, and the very name of "Rich Port," given to it without cause or reason, must have sounded in the ears of the inhabitants as a bitter sarcasm on their wretched condition.

FOOTNOTES:
[Footnote 39: A precarious traffic in hides and ginger did not deserve the name of commerce.]

CHAPTER XIX
ATTACK ON SAN JUAN BY THE HOLLANDERS UNDER BOWDOIN
1625

Holland emancipated itself from Spanish domination in 1582 and assumed the title of "the United Provinces of Netherland." After nearly half a century of an unequal struggle with the most powerful kingdom in Europe, the people's faith in final success was unbounded, while Spain was growing weary of the apparently interminable war. At this juncture, proposals for a suspension of hostilities were willingly entertained by both nations, and after protracted negotiations, a truce of twelve years was signed in Bergen-op-Zoom, April 9, 1609. In it the absolute independence of the United Provinces was recognized.

This gave the Spanish colonies a welcome respite from the ravages of privateers till 1621, the first year of the reign of King Philip IV, when hostilities immediately recommenced. France and England both came to the assistance of the Provinces with money for the raising of troops, and the wealthy merchants of Holland, following the example of the French merchants in the former century, fitted out fleets of privateers to prey upon the commerce and colonies of Spain and Portugal. The first exploits of these privateers were the invasion of Brazil and the sacking of San Salvador, of Lima and Callao (1624).

Puerto Rico was just beginning to recover from the prostration in which the last invasion had left it, when on the morning of the 24th of September, 1625, the guard on San Felipe del Morro announced 8 ships to windward of the port.

Juan de Haro, the governor, who had assumed the command only a few months before, mounted to an outlook to observe them, and was informed that more ships could be seen some distance down the coast. He sent out horsemen, and they returned about 8 o'clock at night with the news that they had counted 17 ships in all.

Alarm-bells were now rung and some cannon fired from the forts to call the inhabitants together. They were directed to the plaza, where arms and ammunition were distributed. During the night the whole city was astir preparing for events, under the direction of the governor.

Next morning the whole fleet was a short distance to windward. Lest a landing should be attempted at the Boquerón or at Goat's Creek, the two most likely places, the governor ordered a cannon to be planted at each and trenches to be dug. In the meantime, the people, who had promptly answered the call to arms, and the garrison were formed into companies on the plaza and received orders to occupy the forts, marching first along the shore, where the enemy could see them, so as to make a great show of numbers.

The artillery in the fort was in bad condition. The gun-carriages were old and rotten. Some of the pieces had been loaded four years before and were dismounted at the first firing. One of them burst on the sixth or seventh day, killing the gunners and severely wounding the governor, who personally superintended the defense.

In the afternoon of the day of their arrival the Hollanders came down under full sail "with as much confidence," says the chronicler, "as if they were entering a port in their own country."

That night the fort was provisioned as well as the scanty resources of the island permitted. The defenders numbered 330, and the food supply collected would not enable them to stand a long siege. The supply consisted of 120 loads of casabe bread, 46 bushels of maize, 130 jars or jugs of olive oil, 10 barrels of biscuit, 300 island cheeses, 1 cask of flour, 30 pitchers of wine, 200 fowls, and 150 small boxes of preserved fruit (membrillo).

Fortunately during the night 50 head of cattle and 20 horses were driven in from the surrounding country.

From the 26th to the 29th the enemy busied himself landing troops, digging trenches, and planting 6 pieces of cannon on a height called "the Calvary." Then he began firing at the fort, which replied, doing considerable damage.

At 9 o'clock on the morning of the 30th, a drummer under a flag of truce presented himself before the castle with a letter addressed to the governor. It was couched in the following terms:

"Señor Governor Don Juan Faro, you must be well aware of the reasons of our coming so near and of our intentions. Therefore, I, Bowdoin Hendrick, general of these forces, in the name of the States General and of his Highness the Prince of Orange, do hereby demand that you deliver this castle and garrison into our hands, which doing we will not fail to come to terms with you. And if not, I give you notice, that from this day forward we will spare neither old nor young, woman nor child; and to this we wait your answer in a few words.

"BOWDOIN HENDRICK."

To which epistle the governor replied:

"I have seen your paper, and am surprised that you should ask such a thing of me, seeing that I have served thirteen years in Flanders, where I have learned to value your boastings and know what sieges are. On the contrary, if you will deliver the ships in which you have come to me, I will let you have one to return with. And these are the orders of my King and Master, and none other, with which I have answered your paper, in the Castle of San Felipe del Morro, the 30th of September, 1625.

"JUAN DE HARO."

The next day a heavy cannonading commenced, the Hollanders firing over 150 shots at the castle with small effect. The same day a Spanish ship arrived with wine and provisions, but seeing the danger it ran of being taken, did not enter the port, but steered to la Española, to the great disappointment of the people in the fort.

On the 4th of October the governor ordered a sortie of 80 men in three parties. On the 5th Captain Juan de Amezquita led another sortie, and so between sorties, surprises, night attacks, and mutual cannonadings things continued till the 21st of October.

On that day Bowdoin sent another letter announcing his intention of burning the city if no understanding was arrived at. To which letter the governor replied that there was building material enough in the island to construct another city, and that he wished the whole army of Holland might be here to witness Spanish bravery.

Bowdoin carried his threat into effect, and the next day over a hundred houses were burned. Bishop Balbueno's palace and library and the city archives were also destroyed. To put a stop to this wanton destruction Captains Amezquita and Botello led a sortie of 200 men. They attacked the enemy in front and rear with such *élan* that they drove them from their trenches and into the water in their haste to reach their launches.

This, and other remarkable exploits, related by the native chroniclers, so discouraged the Hollanders that they abandoned the siege on the 2d of November, leaving behind them one of their largest ships, stranded, and over 400 dead.

The fleet repaired to la Aguáda to refit. Bowdoin, who, apparently, was a better letter writer than general, sent a third missive to the governor, asking permission to purchase victuals, which was, of course, flatly refused.

The king duly recompensed the brave defenders. The governor was made Chevalier of the Order of Santiago and received a money grant of 2,000 ducats. Captain Amezquita received 1,000 ducats, and was later appointed Governor of Cuba. Captain Botello also received 1,000 ducats, and others who had distinguished themselves received corresponding rewards.

Puerto Rico's successful resistance to this invasion encouraged the belief that, provided the mother country should furnish the necessary means of defense, the island would end by commanding the respect of its enemies and be left unmolested. But the mother country's wars with England, France, and Holland absorbed all its attention in Europe and consumed all its resources. The colonies remained dependent for their defense on their own efforts, while privateers, freebooters, and pirates of the three nations at war with Spain settled like swarms of hornets in every available island in the West Indies.

CHAPTER XX
DECLINE OF SPAIN'S POWER—BUCCANEERS AND FILIBUSTERS
1625-1780

The power of Spain received its death-blow during the course of the war with England. The destruction of the Armada and of the fleets subsequently equipped by Philip II for the invasion of Ireland were calamities from which Spain never recovered.

The wars with almost every European nation in turn, which raged during the reigns of the third and fourth Philips, swallowed up all the blood-stained treasure that the colonial governors could wring from the natives of the New World. The flower of the German and Italian legions had left their bones in the marshes of Holland, and Spain, the proudest nation in Europe, had been humiliated to the point of treating for peace, on an equal footing, with a handful of rebels and recognizing their independence. France had four armies in the field against her (1637). A fleet equipped with great sacrifice and difficulty was destroyed by the Hollanders in the waters of Brazil (1630). Van Tromp annihilated another in the English Channel, consisting of 70 ships, with 10,000 of Spain's best troops on board. Cataluña was in open revolt (1640). The Italian provinces followed (1641). Portugal fought and achieved her emancipation from Spanish rule. The treasury was empty, the people starving. Yet, while all these calamities were befalling the land, the king and his court, under the guidance of an inept minister (the Duke of Olivares), were wasting the country's resources in rounds of frivolous and immoral pleasures, in dances, theatrical representations, and bull-fights. The court was corrupt; vice and crime were rampant in the streets of Madrid.[40]

Under such a régime the colonists were naturally left to take care of themselves, and this, coupled with the policy of excluding them from all foreign commerce, justified Spain's enemies in seeking to wrest from her the possessions from which she drew the revenues that enabled her to make war on them. Englishmen, Frenchmen, and Hollanders made of the Antilles their trysting-ground for the purpose of preying upon the common enemy.

These were the buccaneers and filibusters of that period, the most lawless class of men in an age of universal lawlessness, the refuse from the seaports of northern Europe, as cruel miscreants as ever blackened the pages of history.

The buccaneers derived their name from the Carib word "boucan," a kind of gridiron on which, like the natives, they cooked their meat, hence, bou-canier. The word filibuster comes from the Spanish "fee-lee-bote," English "fly-boat," a small, swift sailing-vessel with a large mainsail, which enabled the buccaneers to pursue merchantmen in the open sea and escape among the shoals and shallows of the archipelago when pursued in their turn by men-of-war.

They recognized no authority, no law but force. They obeyed a leader only when on their plundering expeditions. The spoils were equally divided, the captain's share being double that of the men. The maimed in battle received a compensation proportionate to the injury received. The captains were naturally distinguished by the qualities of character that alone could command obedience from crews who feared neither God nor man.

One of the most dreaded among them was a Frenchman, a native of Sables d'Olonne, hence called l'Olonais. He had been a prisoner of the Spaniards, and the treatment he received at their hands had filled his soul with such deadly hatred, that when he regained his liberty he swore a solemn oath to live henceforth for revenge alone. And he did. He never spared sex or age, and took a hellish pleasure in torturing his victims. He made several descents on the coast of this island, burned Maracaibo, Puerto Cabello, Veragua, and other places, and was killed at last by the Indians of Darien.

Sir Henry Morgan, a Welsh aristocrat turned pirate, was another famous scourge of the Spanish colonies. His inhuman treatment of the inhabitants of Puerto Principe, in 1668, is a matter of history. He plundered Porto Bello, Chagres, Panamá, and extended his depredations to the coast of Costa Rica. He used to subject his victims to torture to make them declare where they had hidden their valuables, and many a poor wretch who had no valuables to hide was ruthlessly tortured to death.

Pierre Legrand was another Frenchman who, after committing all kinds of outrages in the West Indies, passed with his robber crew to the Pacific and scoured the coasts as far as California.

The atrocities committed by a certain Montbras, of Languedoc, earned him the name of "the Exterminator."

* * * * *

When the first buccaneers made their appearance in the Antilles (1520), the Windward Islands were still occupied by the Caribs. Here they formed temporary settlements, which, by degrees, grew into permanent pirates' nests. In some of these islands they found large herds of cattle, the progeny of the first few heads introduced by the early Spanish colonists, who afterward abandoned them. In 1625 a party of English and French occupied the island San Cristobal. Four years later Puerto Rico, being well garrisoned at the time, the governor, Enrique Henriquez, fitted out an expedition to dislodge them, in which he succeeded only to make them take up new quarters in Antigua.

The next year the French and English buccaneers who occupied the small island of Tortuga made a descent upon the western part of la Española, called Haiti by the natives (mountainous land), and maintained themselves there till that part of the island was ceded to France by the treaty of Ryswyk, in 1697.

Spain equipped a fleet to clear the West Indies from pirates in 1630, and placed it under the command of Don Federico de Toledo. He was met in the neighborhood of San Cristobal by a numerous fleet of small craft, which had the advantage over the unwieldy Spanish ships in that they could maneuver with greater rapidity and precision. There are no reliable details of the result of the engagement. Abbad tells us that the Spaniards were victorious, but the buccaneers continued to occupy all the islands which they had occupied before.

In 1634 they took possession of Curagao, Aruba, and Bonaíre, near the coast of Venezuela, and established themselves in 1638 in San Eustaquio, Saba, San Martin, and Santa Cruz.

In 1640 the Governor of Puerto Rico sought to expel them from the last-named island. He defeated them, killing many and taking others prisoners; but as soon as he returned to Puerto Rico the Hollanders from San Eustaquio and San Martin reoccupied Santa Cruz, and he was compelled to equip another expedition to dislodge them, in which he was completely successful. This time he left a garrison, but in the same year the French commander, Poincy, came with a strong force and compelled the garrison to capitulate. The island remained a French possession under the name of Saint Croix until it was sold to Denmark, in 1733, for $150,000. Another expedition set out from Puerto Rico in 1650, to oust the French and Hollanders from San Martin. The Spaniards destroyed a fort that had been constructed there, but as soon as they returned to this island the pirates reoccupied their nest. In 1657 an Englishman named Cook came with a sufficient force and San Martin became an English possession.

About 1665 the French Governor of Tortuga, Beltrán Ogeron, planned the conquest of Puerto Rico. He appeared off the coast with 3 ships, but one of the hurricanes so frequent in these latitudes came to the island's rescue. The ships were stranded, and the surviving Frenchmen made prisoners. Among them was Ogeron himself, but his men shielded him by saying that he was drowned. On the march to the capital he and his ship's surgeon managed to escape, and, after killing the owner of a fishing-smack, returned to Tortuga, where he immediately commenced preparations for another invasion of Puerto Rico. When he came back he was so well received by the armed peasantry (jíbaros) that he was forced to reembark.

From this time to 1679 several expeditions were fitted out in San Juan to drive the filibusters from one or another of the islands in the neighborhood. In 1780 a fleet was equipped with the object of definitely destroying all the pirates' nests. The greater part of the garrison, all the Puerto Ricans most distinguished for bravery, intelligence, and experience, took part in the expedition. The fleet was accompanied by the Spanish battle-ship Carlos V, which carried 50 cannon and 500 men. Of this expedition not a soul returned. It was totally destroyed by a hurricane, and the island was once more plunged in mourning, ruin, and poverty, from which it did not emerge till nearly a century later.

FOOTNOTES:

[Footnote 40: In fifteen days 110 men and women were assassinated in the capital alone, some of them persons of distinction. Cánovas, Decadencia de España, Libro VI.]

CHAPTER XXI
BRITISH ATTACKS ON PUERTO RICO—SIEGE OF SAN JUAN BY SIR RALPH ABERCROMBIE

1678-1797

The *entente cordiale* which had existed between England under Charles I and Spain under Philip IV ceased with the tragic death of the first-named monarch. [41]

Immediately after Cromwell's elevation both France and Spain made overtures for an alliance with England. But the Protector well knew that in the event of war with either power, Spain's colonies and treasure-laden galleons offered a better chance for obtaining booty than the poor possessions of France. He favored an alliance with Louis XIV, and ended by signing a treaty with him in 1657.

The first result of the hostilities that ensued was the capture by the English Admirals Blake and Stayner of several richly laden galleons.

From that time to the end of the eighteenth century England's attempts to secure the two most-coveted Antilles (Cuba and Puerto Rico) continued with short intervals of peace.

In 1768 an English fleet of 22 ships, with a landing force under the command of the Earl of Estren, appeared before San Juan and demanded its surrender. Before a formal attack could be made a furious hurricane wrecked the fleet on Bird Island, and everybody on board perished excepting a few soldiers and marines, who escaped a watery grave only to be made prisoners.[42]

It is certain, however, that on August 5, 1702, an English brigantine and a sloop came to Arecibo and landed 30 men, who were forced to reembark with considerable loss, though the details of this affair, as given by Friar Abbad, and repeated by Mr. Neuman, are evidently largely drawn from imagination.

In September of the following year (1703) there were landings of Englishmen near Loiza and in the neighborhood of San German, of which we know only that they were stoutly opposed; and we learn from an official document that there was another landing at Boca Chica on the south coast in 1743, when the English were once more obliged to reembark with the loss of a pilot-boat.

These incessant attacks, not on Puerto Rico only, but on all the other Spanish possessions, and the reprisals they provoked, created such animosity between the people of both countries that hostilities had practically commenced before the declaration of war (October 23, 1739). In November Admiral Vernon was already in the Antilles with a large fleet. He took Porto Bello, laid siege to Cartagena, but was forced to withdraw; then he made an ineffectual attack on Cuba, after which he passed round Cape Horn into the Pacific, caused great consternation in Chile, sacked and burned Payta, captured the galleon Covadonga with a cargo worth $1,500,000, and finally returned to England with a few ships only and less than half his men.

The next war between the two nations was the result of the famous Bourbon family compact, and lasted from 1761 to 1763.

Two powerful fleets sailed from England for the Antilles; the one under the orders of Admiral Rodney attacked the French colonies and took Martinique,

Granada, Santa Lucia, San Vicente, and Tabago; the other under Admiral Pocock appeared before Havana, June 2, 1762, with a fleet of 30 line-of-battle ships, 100 transports, and 14,000 landing troops under the command of the Earl of Albemarle. In four days the English took "la Cabaña," which Prado, the governor, considered the key to the city. For some unexplained reason the Spanish fleet became useless; but Captain Louis Velasco defended the Morro, and for two months and ten days he kept the English at bay, till they undermined the walls of the fort and blew them up. Then Prado capitulated (August 13), and Havana with its forts and defenses, with 60 leagues of territory to the west of the city, with $15,000,000, an immense quantity of naval and military stores, 9 line-of-battle ships and 3 frigates, was delivered into Albemarle's hands. It was Puerto Rico's turn next, and preparations were made for an attack, when the signing of the treaty of peace in Paris (February, 1763) averted the imminent danger.

By the stipulations of that treaty England returned Havana and Manila[43] to Spain in exchange for Florida and some territories on the Mississippi; she also returned to France part of her conquered possessions.

In 1778 Charles III joined France in a war against England, the motives for which, as explained by the king's minister, were frivolous in the extreme. The real reason was England's refusal to admit Spain as mediator in the differences with her North American colonies. This war lasted till 1783, and though the Antilles, as usual, became the principal scene of war, Puerto Rico happily escaped attack.

Not so during the hostilities that broke out anew in consequence of Charles IV's offensive and defensive alliance with the French Republic, signed in San Ildefonso on the 18th of August, 1796.

In February, 1797, Admiral Henry Harvey, with 60 ships, including transports and small craft, and from 6,000 to 7,000 troops under the orders of Sir Ralph Abercrombie, appeared before the island of Trinidad and took possession of it with but little resistance from the Spanish garrison. On the 17th of April the whole fleet appeared before San Juan.

The capital was well prepared for defense. The forts, as now existing, were completed, and the city surrounded by a wall the strength of which may be estimated by the appearance of the parts still intact. On these defenses 376 pieces of cannon of different caliber were planted, besides 35 mortars, 4 howitzers, and 3 swivel guns. The garrison was reduced to about 200 men, part of the troops having been sent to la Española to quell the insurrection of the negro population led by Toussaint L'Ouverture. There were, besides these 200 veteran troops, 4,000 militiamen, about 2,000 men from the towns in the interior (urbános) armed with lances and machetes, 12 gunboats and several French privateers, the crews of which numbered about 300.

Abercrombie landed on the 18th at Cangrejos (Santurce) with 3,000 men, and demanded the surrender of the city. Governor Castro, in polite but energetic language, refused, and hostilities commenced. For the next thirteen days there were skirmishes and more or less serious encounters on land and sea. On the morning of the 1st of May the defenders of the city were preparing a general attack on the English lines, when, lo! the enemy had reembarked during the night, leaving behind his spiked guns and a considerable quantity of stores and ammunition.

The people ascribed this unexpected deliverance from their foes to the miraculous intervention of the Virgin, but the real reason for the raising of the siege was the strength of the fortifications. "Whoever has viewed these fortifications," says Colonel Flinter,[44] "must feel surprised that the English with a force of less than 5,000 men should lay siege to the place, a force not sufficient for a single line along the coast on the opposite side of the bay to prevent provisions from being sent to the garrison from the surrounding country. Sir Ralph's object in landing, surely, could only have been to try whether he could surprise or intimidate the scanty garrison. Had he not reembarked very soon, he would have had to repent his temerity, for the shipping could not safely remain at anchor where there was no harbor and where a dangerous coast threatened destruction. His communication with the country was cut off by the armed peasantry, who rose *en masse*, and to the number of not less than 20,000 threw themselves into the fortress in less than a week after the invasion, so that the British forces would, most undoubtedly, have been obliged to surrender at discretion had the commander not effected a timely retreat."

The enemy's retreat was celebrated with a solemn Te Deum in the cathedral, at which the governor, the municipal authorities, and all the troops assisted. The municipality addressed the king, giving due credit to the brilliant military qualities displayed during the siege by the governor and his officers. The governor was promoted to the rank of field-marshal and the officers correspondingly. To the municipality the privilege was granted to encircle the city's coat of arms with the words: "For its constancy, love, and fidelity, this city is yclept very noble and very loyal."

FOOTNOTES:

[Footnote 41: He was decapitated February 9, 1649.]

[Footnote 42: So says Abbad. No mention is made of this episode in Señor Acosta's notes, nor is the name of Earl Estren to be found among those of the British commanders of that period.]

[Footnote 43: Manila was taken in October, 1762.]

[Footnote 44: An Account of Puerto Rico. London, 1834.]

CHAPTER XXII

BRITISH ATTACKS ON PUERTO RICO *(continued)*—INVASIONS BY COLOMBIAN INSURGENTS

1797-1829

The raising of the siege of San Juan by Abercrombie did not raise at the same time the blockade of the island. Communications with the metropolis were cut off, and the remittances from Mexico which, under the appellation of "situados," constituted the only means of carrying on the Government, were suspended.[45] In San Juan the garrison was kept on half pay, provisions were scarce, and the influx of immigrants from la Española, where a bloody civil war raged at the time, increased the consumption and the price. The militia corps was disbanded to prevent serious injury to the island's agricultural interests, although English attacks on different points of the coast continued, and kept the inhabitants in a state of constant fear and alarm.

In December, 1797, an English three-decker and a frigate menaced Aguadilla, but an attempt at landing was repulsed. Another attempt to land was made at Guayanilla with the same result, and in June, 1801, Guayanilla was again attacked. This time an English frigate sent several launches full of men ashore, but they were beaten off by the people, who, armed only with lances and machetes, pursued them into the water, "swimming or wading up to their necks," says Mr. Neuman.[46]

From 1801 to 1808 England's navy and English privateers pursued both French and Spanish ships with dogged pertinacity. In August, 1803, British privateers boarded and captured a French frigate in the port of Salinas in this island. Four Spanish homeward-bound frigates fell into their hands about the same time. Another English frigate captured a French privateer in what is now the port of Ponce (November 12, 1804) and rescued a British craft which the privateer had captured. Even the negroes of Haiti armed seven privateers under British auspices and preyed upon the French and Spanish merchant ships in these Antilles.

Governor Castro, during the whole of his period of service, had vainly importuned the home Government for money and arms and ships to defend this island against the ceaseless attacks of the English. When he handed over the command to his successor, Field-Marshal Toribio Montes, in 1804, the treasury was empty. He himself had long ceased to draw his salary, and the money necessary to attend to the most pressing needs for the defense was obtained by contributions from the inhabitants.

While the people of Puerto Rico were thus giving proofs of their loyalty to Spain, and sacrificing their lives and property to preserve their poverty-stricken island to the Spanish crown, the other colonies, rich and important, were breaking the bonds that united them to the mother country.

The example of the English colonies had long since awakened among the more enlightened class of creoles on the continent a desire for emancipation, which the events in France on the one hand, and the ill-advised, often cruel measures adopted by the Spanish authorities to quench that aspiration, on the other hand, had only served to make irresistible. But Puerto Rico did not aspire to emancipation. It never had been a colony, there was no creole class, and the only indigenous population—the "jíbaros," the mixed descendants of Indians, negroes, and Spaniards—were too poor, too illiterate, too ignorant of everything concerning the outside world to look with anything but suspicion upon the invitations of the insurgents of Colombia and Venezuela to join them or imitate their example. They, nor the great majority of the masses whom Bolivar, San Martin, Hidalgo, and others liberated from an oppressive yoke, cared little for the rights of man. When the Colombian insurgents landed on the coast of Puerto Rico, to encourage and assist the people to shake off a yoke which did not gall them, they were looked upon by the natives as freebooters of another class who came to plunder them.

On the 20th of December, 1819, an insurgent brigantine and a sloop attempted a landing at Aguadilla. They were beaten back by a Spanish sergeant at the head of a detachment of twenty men, while a Mr. Domeneck with his servants attended to the artillery in Fort San Carlos, constructed during Castro's administration. In February, 1825, some insurgent ships landed fifty marines at night near Point Boriquén, where the lighthouse now is. They captured the fort by surprise and dismounted the guns, but the people of Aguadilla replaced them on their carriages the next day and offered such energetic resistance to the landing parties that they had to retreat.

Another landing was effected at Patillas in November, 1829. This port was opened to commerce by royal decree December 30, 1821. There were several small trading craft in the port at the time of the attack. They fell a prey to the invaders; but when they landed they were met by the armed inhabitants, and after a sharp fight, in which the Colombians had 8 men killed, they reembarked.

* * * * *

The beginning of the nineteenth century found Spain deprived of all that beautiful island world which Columbus had laid at the foot of the throne of Ferdinand and Isabel four centuries ago, of all but a part of the "Española," since called Santo Domingo, and of the two Antilles. Before the first quarter of the century had passed all the continental colonies had broken the bonds that united them to the mother country, and before the twentieth century the last vestiges of the most extensive and the richest colonial empire ever possessed by any nation refused further allegiance, as the logical result of four centuries of political, religious, and financial myopia.

FOOTNOTES:

[Footnote 45: They ceased altogether in 1810, as a result of the revolution in Mexico.]

[Footnote 46: Benefactores and Hombres Illustres de Puerto Rico, p. 289.]

CHAPTER XXIII
REVIEW OF THE SOCIAL CONDITIONS IN PUERTO RICO AND THE POLITICAL EVENTS IN SPAIN FROM
1765 TO 1820

After the conquest of Mexico and Peru with their apparently inexhaustible mineral wealth, Spain attached very little importance to the archipelago of the Antilles. The largest and finest only of these islands were selected for colonization, the small and comparatively sterile ones were neglected, and fell an easy prey to pirates and privateers.

Puerto Rico, notwithstanding its advantages of soil and situation, was considered for the space of three centuries only as a fit place of banishment (a *presidio*) for the malefactors of the mother country. Agriculture did not emerge from primitive simplicity. The inhabitants led a pastoral life, cultivating food barely sufficient for their support, because there was no stimulus to exertion.

They looked passively upon the riches centered in their soil, and rocked themselves to sleep in their hammocks. The commerce carried on scarcely deserved that name. The few wants of the people were supplied by a contraband trade with St. Thomas and Santa Cruz. In the island's finances a system of fraud and peculation prevailed, and the amount of public revenue was so inadequate to meet the expenses of maintaining the garrison that the officers' and soldiers' pay was reduced to one-fourth of its just amount, and they often received only a miserable ration.

His Excellency Alexander O'Reilly, who came to the Antilles on a commission from Charles IV, in his report on Puerto Rico (1765) gives the following description of the condition of the inhabitants at that time:

" ... To form an idea of how these natives have lived and still live, it is enough to say that there are only two schools in the whole island; that outside of the capital and San German few know how to read; that they count time by changes in the Government, hurricanes, visits from bishops, arrivals of 'situados,' etc. They do not know what a league is. Each one reckons distance according to his own speed in traveling. The principal ones among them, including those of the capital, when they are in the country go barefooted and barelegged. The whites show no reluctance at being mixed up with the colored population. In the towns (the capital included) there are few permanent inhabitants besides the curate; the others are always in the country, except Sundays and feast-days, when those living near to where there is a church come to hear mass. During these feast-days they occupy houses that look like hen-coops. They consist of a couple of rooms, most of them without doors or windows, and therefore open day and night. Their furniture is so scant that they can move in an instant. The country houses are of the same description. There is little distinction among the people. The only difference between them consists in the possession of a little more or less property, and, perhaps, the rank of a subaltern officer in the militia."

Abbad makes some suggestions for increasing the population. He proposes the distribution of the unoccupied lands among the "agregados" or idle "hangers-on" of each family; among the convicts who have served out their time and can not or will not return to the Peninsula; among the freed slaves, who have purchased their own freedom or have been manumitted by their masters; and, finally, among the great number of individuals who, having deserted from ships or being left behind, wandered about from place to place or became contrabandists, pirates, or thieves.

"Their numbers are so small and the soil so fruitful they generally have an abundance of bananas, maize, beans, and other food. Fish is abundant, and few are without a cow or two. The only furniture they have and need is a hammock and a cooking-pot. Plates, spoons, jugs, and basins they make of the bark of the 'totumo,' a tree which is found in every forest. A saber or a 'machete,' as they call it, is the only agricultural implement they use. The construction of their houses does not occupy them more than a day or two."

The good friar goes on to tell us that, through indolence, they have not even learned from the Indians how to protect their plantations from the fierce heat of the sun and avoid consequent failure of crops in time of drought, by making the

69

plantations in clearings in the forest, so that the surrounding walls of verdure may give moisture and shade to the plants. "Nor have they learned to build their bohíos (huts) to windward of swamps or clearings to avoid the fever-laden emanations."

* * * * *

The stirring events in Europe that marked the end of the eighteenth and the beginning of the nineteenth centuries did not find these conditions much changed, though *some* advance had been made and was being made in spite of the prohibitive measures of the Government, which were well calculated to check all advance. To prevent the spread of the ideas that had given birth to the French Revolution, absolute powers were granted to the captains-general, odious restrictions were placed upon all communication with the interior, sacrifices in men and money were demanded on the plea of patriotism, and a policy of suspicion and distrust adopted toward the colonies which in the end fomented the very political aspirations it was intended to suppress.

From the outbreak of the French Revolution, Spain was entangled in a maze of political difficulties. The natural sympathy of Charles IV for the unfortunate King of France well-nigh provoked hostilities between the two nations from the very beginning. The king gave public expression to his opinion that to make war on France was as legitimate as to make war on pirates and bandits; and the Directory, though it took little notice at the time, remembered it when Godoy, the favorite, in his endeavors to save the lives of Louis XVI and his family entered into correspondence with the French emigres. Then war was declared.

The war was popular. All classes contended to make the greatest sacrifices to aid the Government. Men and money came in abundantly, and before long three army corps crossed the Pyrenees into French territory ... They had to recross the next year, followed by the victorious soldiers of the Republic, who planted the tricolor on some of the principal Spanish frontier fortresses. Then the peace of Basilia was signed, and, as one of the conditions of that peace, Spain ceded to France the part she still held of Santo Domingo.

From this period Charles, in the terror inspired by the excesses of the Revolution and the probable fear for his own safety, forgot that he was a Bourbon and began to seek an alliance with the executioners of his family. As a result, the treaty of San Ildefonso was signed (1796). Spain became the enemy of England, and the first effects thereof which she experienced were the bombardment of Cadiz by an English fleet, the loss of the island of Trinidad, and the siege of Puerto Rico by Abercrombie.

Spain also became the willing vassal, rather than the ally, of the military genius whom the French Revolution had revealed, and obeyed his mandates without a murmur. In 1803 Napoleon demanded a subsidy of 6,000,000 francs per month as the price of Spain's neutrality, but in the following year he insisted on the renewal of the alliance against England (treaty of Paris, 1804). The total destruction of the Spanish fleet at the battles of Saint Vincent and Trafalgar was the result.

Godoy, who in his ambitious dreams had seen a crown and a throne somewhere in Portugal to be bestowed on him by the man to whose triumphal car he had attached his king and his country, began to suspect Napoleon's intentions.

Seeing the war-clouds gather in the north of Europe, he thought that the coalition of the powers against the tyrant was the presage of his downfall, and he now hastened to send an emissary to England.

The war-clouds burst, and from amid the thunder and smoke of battle at Jena, Eylau, and Friedland, the victor's figure arose more imperious than ever. All the crowned heads of Europe but one[47] hastened to do him homage, among them Charles IV of Spain and the Prince of Asturias, his son.

The next step in the grand drama that was being enacted was the occupation of Spanish territory by what Bonaparte was pleased to call an army of observation. This time Godoy's suspicions became confirmed, and to save the royal family he counsels the king to withdraw to Andalusia. Ferdinand conspires to dethrone his father, the people become excited, riots take place, Godoy's residence in Aranguez is attacked by the mob, and the king abdicates in favor of his son. Napoleon himself now lands at Bayona. Charles and his son hasten thither to salute Europe's master, and, after declaring that his abdication was imposed on him by violence, the king resumes his crown and humbly lays it at the feet of the arbiter of the fate of kings, who stoops to pick it up only to offer it to his brother Louis, who refuses it. Then he places it on the head of his younger brother Joseph.

Thus fared the crown of Spain, the erstwhile proud mistress of half the world, and the degenerate successors of Charles V accept an asylum in France from the hands of a soldier of fortune.

But if their rulers had lost all sense of dignity, all feeling of national pride, the Spanish nation remained true to itself, and when the doings at Bayona became known a cry of indignation went up from the Pyrenees to the Mediterranean. On May 2, 1808, the people of Spain commenced a six years' struggle full of heroic and terrible episodes. At the end of that period the necessity of withdrawing the French troops from Spain to confront the second coalition, and the assistance of the English under Lord Wellesley cleared the Peninsula of French soldiers. After the battle of Leipzig (1813) a treaty between Ferdinand VII and Napoleon was signed in Valencia, and Spain's independence was recognized and guaranteed by the allies.

* * * * *

From the beginning of the war many officers and privates, residents of Puerto Rico, enlisted to serve against the French, and large sums of money, considering the island's poverty, were subscribed among the inhabitants to aid in the defense of the mother country.

Ferdinand VII reentered Madrid as king on March 24, 1814, accompanied by a coterie of retrograde, revengeful priests, of whom his confessor, Victor Saez, was the leader. He made this priest Minister of State, and soon proved the truth of the saying that the Bourbons forget nothing, forgive nothing, and learn nothing from experience.

He commenced by ignoring the regency and the Cortes. These had preserved his kingdom for him while he was an exile. He refused to recognize the constitution which they had framed, and at once initiated an epoch of cruel persecution against such as had distinguished themselves by their talents, love of liberty, and progressive ideas. The public press was completely silenced, the Inquisition reestablished, the convents reopened, provincial deputations and municipalities abolished, distinguished men were surprised in their beds at night and torn from the arms of their wives and children, to be conducted by soldiers to the fortress of Ceuta—in short, the Government was a civil dictatorship occupied in hanging the most distinguished citizens, while the military authorities busied themselves in shooting them.

In the colonies the king's lackeys repeated the same outrages. Puerto Rico suffered like the rest, and many of the best families emigrated to the neighboring English and French possessions.

The result of the royal turpitude was the revolution headed by Rafael Diego, seconded by General O'Daly, a Puerto Rican by birth, who had greatly distinguished himself in the war against the French. Other generals and their troops followed, and when General Labisbal, sent by Ferdinand to quell the insurrection, joined his comrades, the trembling tyrant was only too glad to save his throne by swearing to maintain the constitution of 1812. O'Daly's share in these events raised him to the rank of field-marshal, and the people of Puerto Rico elected him their deputy to Cortes by a large majority (1820).

The first constitutional régime in Puerto Rico was not abolished till December 3, 1814. For the great majority of the inhabitants of the island at that time the privileges of citizenship had neither meaning nor value. They were still too profoundly ignorant, too desperately poor, to take any interest in what was passing outside of their island. Cock-fighting and horse-racing occupied most of their time. Schools had not increased much since O'Reilly reported the existence of two in 1765. There was an official periodical, the Gazette, in which the Government offered spelling-books *for sale* to those who wished to learn to read. [48]

During the second constitutional period, Puerto Rico was divided by a resolution in Cortes into 7 judicial districts, and tablets with the constitutional prescriptions on them were ordered to be placed in the plazas of the towns in the interior. Public spirit began to awaken, several patriotic associations were formed, among them those of "the Lovers of Science," "the Liberals, Lovers of their Country," and others. But the dawn of progress was eclipsed again toward the end of 1823, when the news of the fall of the second constitutional régime reached Puerto Rico a few months after the people had elected their deputies to Cortes.

FOOTNOTES:

[Footnote 47: The King of England.]

[Footnote 48: Neuman, p. 354.]

CHAPTER XXIV
GENERAL CONDITION OF THE ISLAND
FROM 1815 TO 1833

That Ferdinand should, while engaged in cruel persecution of his best subjects in the Peninsula, think of dictating liberal laws for this island is an anomaly which can be explained only by its small political importance.

In August, 1815, there appeared a decree entitled "Regulations for promoting the population, commerce, industry, and agriculture of Puerto Rico." It embraced every object, and provided for all the various incidents that could instil life and vigor into an infant colony. It held out the most flattering prospects to industrious and enterprising foreigners. It conferred the rights and privileges of Spaniards on them and their children. Lands were granted to them gratis, and no expenses attended the issue of titles and legal documents constituting it private property. The quantity of land allotted was in proportion to the number of slaves introduced by each new settler. The new colonists were not to be subject to taxes or export duty on their produce, or import duties on their agricultural implements. If war should be declared between Spain and their native country, their persons and properties were to be respected, and if they wished to leave the island they were permitted to realize on their property and carry its value along with them, paying 10 per cent on the surplus of the capital they had brought. They were exempted from the capitation tax or personal tribute. Each slave was to pay a tax of one dollar yearly after having been ten years in the island. During the first five years the colonists had liberty to return to their former places of residence, and in this case could carry with them all that they had brought without being obliged to pay export duty. Those who should die in the island without heirs might leave their property to their friends and relations in other countries. The heirs had the privilege of remaining on the same conditions as the testators, or if they preferred to take away their inheritance they might do so on paying a duty of 15 per cent.

The colonists were likewise exonerated from the payment of tithes for fifteen years, and at the end of that period they were to pay only 2 12 per cent. They were equally free, for the same period, from the payment of alcabala,[49] and at the expiration of the specified term they were to pay 2 12 per cent, but if they shipped their produce to Spain, nothing. The introduction of negroes into the island was to be perpetually free. Direct commerce with Spain and the other Spanish possessions was to be free for fifteen years, and after that period Puerto Rico was to be placed on the same footing with the other Spanish colonies. These concessions and exemptions were contained in thirty-three articles, and though, at the present day, they may seem but the abolition of unwarrantable abuses, at the time the concessions were made they were real and important and produced salutary effects. They brought foreigners possessing capital and agricultural knowledge into the country, whose habits of industry and skill in cultivation soon began to be imitated and acquired by the natives.

The effects of the revolution of 1820 were felt in Puerto Rico as well as in Spain. The concentration of civil and military power in the hands of the captains-general ceased, but party spirit began to show its disturbing influence. The press, hitherto muffled by political and ecclesiastical censors, often went to the extremes of abuse and personalities. Mechanics and artisans began to neglect their workshops to listen to the harangues of politicians on the nature of governments and laws. Agriculture and commerce diminished. Great but ineffectual efforts were made to induce the people of Puerto Rico to follow the example of the colonies on the continent and proclaim their independence.

This state of affairs lasted till 1823, when, through French intervention, the constitutional Government in Spain was overthrown, and a second reactionary period set in even worse in its manifestations of odium to progress and liberty than the one of 1814. The leading men of the fallen government, to escape death or imprisonment, emigrated. Among them was O'Daly, who, after living some time in London, settled in Saint Thomas, where he earned a precarious living as teacher of languages.[50]

* * * * *

In 1825 the island's governor was Lieutenant-General Miguel de la Torre, Count de Torrepando, who was invested by the king with viceregal powers, which he used in the first place to put a stop to the organized system of defalcation that existed. The proof of the efficacy of the timely and vigorous proceedings which he employed was the immediate increase of the public revenue, which from that day continued rapidly to advance. The troops in garrison and all persons employed in the public service were regularly paid, nearly half the arrears of back pay were gradually paid off, confidence was restored, and "more was accomplished for the island during the last seven years of Governor La Torre's administration (from 1827 to 1834), and more money arising from its revenues was expended on works of public utility, than the total amounts furnished for the same object during the preceding 300 years." [51]

The era of prosperity which marked the period of Count de Torrepando's administration, and which at the same time prevailed in Cuba also, was largely due to the advent in these Antilles of many of the best and wealthiest citizens of Venezuela, Colombia, and Santo Domingo, who, driven from their homes by the incessant revolutions, to escape persecution settled in them, and infused a new and healthier element in the lower classes of the population.

The condition of Puerto Rican society at this period, though much improved since 1815, still left much to be desired. The leaders of society were the Spanish civil and military officers, who, with little prospect of returning to the Peninsula, married wealthy creole women and made the island their home. Their descendants form the aristocracy of today. Next came the merchants and shopkeepers, active and industrious Catalans, Gallegos, Mallorquins, who seldom married but returned to the Peninsula as soon as they had made sufficient money. These and the soldiers of the garrison made a transitory population. Tradesmen and artisans, as a rule, were creoles. Besides these, the island swarmed with adventurers of all countries, who came and went as fortune favored or frowned.

There was another class of "whites" who made up no inconsiderable portion of the population—namely, the convicts who had served out their time in the island's fortress. Few of them had any inducements to return to their native land. They generally succeeded in finding a refuge with some family of colored people, and it may be supposed that this ingraftment did not enhance the morality of the class with whom they mixed. The evil reputation which Puerto Rico had in the French and English Antilles as being an island where rape, robbery, and assassination were rife was probably due to this circumstance, and not altogether undeserved, for we read[52] that in 1827 the municipal corporation of Aguadilla discussed the convenience of granting or refusing permission for the celebration of the annual Feast of the Conception, which had been suspended since 1820 at the request of the curate, "on account of the gambling, rapes, and robberies that accompanied it."

Horse-racing and cock-fighting remained the principal amusement of the populace. Every house and cabin had its game-cock, every village its licensed cockpit. The houses of all classes were built of wood; the cabins of the "jíbaros" were mere bamboo hovels, where the family, males and females of all ages, slept huddled together on a platform of boards. There were no inns in country or town, except one in the capital. Schools for both sexes were wanting, a few youths were sent by their parents to be educated in France or Spain or the United States, and after two or three years returned with a little superficial knowledge.

About this time the formation of a militia corps of 7,000 men was a step in the right direction. The people, dispersed over the face of the country, living in isolated houses, had little incentive to industry. Their wants were few and easily satisfied, and their time was spent swinging in a hammock or in their favorite amusements. The obligation to serve in the militia forced them to abandon their indolent and unsocial habits and appear in the towns on Sundays for drill. They were thus compelled to be better dressed, and a salutary spirit of emulation was produced. This created new wants, which had to be supplied by increased labor, their manners were softened, and if their morals did not gain, they were, at least, aroused from the listless inactivity of an almost savage life to exertion and social intercourse.

Such were the social conditions of the island when the death of Ferdinand VII gave rise to an uninterrupted succession of political upheavals, the baneful effects of which were felt here.

FOOTNOTES:

[Footnote 49: Duty on the sale of produce or articles of commerce.]

[Footnote 50: In 1834 the Queen Regent, Maria Christina, gave him permission to reside in Puerto Rico. Two years later he was reinstated in favor and was made Military Governor of Cartagena. He died in Madrid a few years later.]

[Footnote 51: Colonel Flinter. An Account of the Present State of the Island of Puerto Rico. London, 1834.]

[Footnote 52: Brau, p. 284.]

CHAPTER XXV
POLITICAL EVENTS IN SPAIN AND THEIR INFLUENCE ON AFFAIRS IN PUERTO RICO
1833-1874

THE French Revolution of 1830 and the expulsion of Charles X revived the hopes of the liberal party in Spain, which party the bigoted absolutism of the king and his minister had vainly endeavored to exterminate. The liberals saluted that event as a promise that the nineteenth century should see the realization of their aspirations, and the exiled members of the party at once came to France to attempt an invasion of Spain, counting upon the sympathy of the French Government, which was denied them. The attempt only brought renewed persecution to the members at home.

Fortunately, the king's failing health and subsequent death transferred the reins of government to the hands of the queen, who, less absolutist than her consort, reopened the universities, which had long been closed, and proclaimed a general amnesty, thus bringing the expatriated and imprisoned Liberals back to political life.

After the king's death the pretensions of Don Carlos, his brother, lit the torch of civil war, which blazed fiercely till 1836, when a revolution changed the Government's policy and the constitution of 1812 was again declared in force. In 1837 the Cortes, though nearly all the Deputies were Progressists, by a vote of 90 to 60, deprived Cuba and Puerto Rico of the right of representation.

Another Carlist campaign was initiated in 1838. In 1839 Maria Christina, having lost her prestige, was obliged to abdicate; then followed the regency of the Duke de la Victoria Espartero, an insurrection in Barcelona, the Cortes of 1843, an attack on Madrid, and the fall of the regency, a period of seven years marked by a series of military pronunciamentos, the last of which was headed by General Prim.

Isabel II was now declared of age (1843), and from the date of her accession two political parties, the Progressists and the Moderates, under the leadership of Espartero and Narvaez respectively, contended for control, until, in 1865, the insurrection of Vicalvaro gave the direction of affairs to O'Donnell, Canovas del Castillo, and others, who represented the liberal Unionist party. They remained in power till 1866, when Prim and Gonzales Bravo raised the standard of revolt once more and Isabel II was dethroned. Then another provisional government was formed under a triumvirate composed of Generals Prim, Serrano, and Topete, who represented the Progressist and the democratic parties (September, 1868). They steered the ship of state till 1871, and, seeing the rocks of revolution still ahead, offered the Spanish crown to Amadeo, who, after wearing it scarce two years, found it too heavy for his brow, and abdicated. He had changed ministeriums six times in less than two years, and came to the conclusion that the modern Spaniards were ungovernable.

A republican form of government was now established (February 11, 1873), and it was understood by all parties that it should be a Federal Republic, in which each of the provinces should enjoy the largest possible amount of autonomy, subject to the authority of the central government.

This proved to be the stumbling-block; the deputies could not agree on the details, passions were aroused, violent discussions took place. The Carlists, seeing a favorable opportunity, plunged the Basque provinces, Navarra, Cataluña, lower Aragón, and part of Castilla and Valencia, into civil war. At the same time, the Radicals promoted what were called "cantonnal" insurrections in Cartagena, and Spain seemed on the verge of social chaos and ruin.

A *coup d'état* saved the country. General Pavia, the Captain-General of Madrid, with a body of guards forced an entrance into the halls of congress and turned the Deputies out (January 3, 1874). A provisional government was once more constituted with Serrano at the head. His first act was to dissolve the Cortes.

* * * * *

The events just summarized exercised a baneful influence on the social, political, and economic conditions of this and of its more important sister Antilla.

Royalists, Carlists, Liberals, Reformists, Unionists, Moderates, and men of other political parties disputed over the direction of the nation's affairs at the point of the sword, and as each party obtained an ephemeral victory it hastened to send its partizans to govern these islands. The new governors invariably proceeded at once to undo what their predecessors had wrought before them.

They succeeded each other at short intervals. From 1837 to 1874 twenty-six captains-general came to Puerto Rico, only six of whom left any grateful memories behind. The others looked upon the people as always watching for an opportunity to follow the example of the continental colonies. They pursued a policy of distrust, suspicion, and of uncompromising antagonism to the people's most legitimate aspirations.

The reactionists, in their implacable odium of progress and liberty, considered every measure calculated to give greater freedom to the people or raise their moral and intellectual status as a crime against the mother country; hence the utter absence of the means of education, and a systematic demoralization of the masses.

Don Angel Acosta[53] mentions the Count de Torrepando as an example of this. He came from Venezuela to govern this island in 1837, with the express purpose, he declared, of diverting the attention of the inhabitants from the revolutionary doings of Bolivar.

Gambling was, and is still, one of the ruling vices of the common people. He encouraged it, established cockpits in every town and instituted the carnival games. He also established the feast of San Juan, which lasted, and still lasts, the whole month of June; and when some respectable people, Insulars as well as Peninsulars, protested against this official propaganda of vice and idleness, he replied: "Let them be—while they dance and gamble they don't conspire; ... these people must be governed by three B's—Barraja, Botella, and Berijo." [54] General Pezuela, a man of liberal disposition and literary attainments,[55] stigmatized the people of Puerto Rico as a people without faith, without thought, and without religion, and, though he afterward did something for the intellectual development of the inhabitants, in the beginning of his administration (1848-1851) thought it expedient not to discourage cock-fighting, but regulated it.

In 1865 gambling was public and universal. In the capital there was a gambling-house in almost every street. One in the upper story of the house at the corner of San Francisco and Cruz Streets, kept by an Italian, was crowded day and night. The bank could be distinctly seen from the Plaza, and the noise, the oaths, the foul language, mixing with the chink of money distinctly heard. When the governor's attention (General Felix Messina) was called to the scandalous exhibition, his answer was: "Let them gamble, ... while they are at it they will not occupy themselves with politics, and if they get ruined it is for the benefit of others."

This systematic villification of the people completely neutralized the effect of the measures adopted from time to time by progressist governors, such as the Count of Mirasol, Norzagaray, Cotoner, and Pavia, and not even the revolution of September, 1868, materially affected the disgraceful condition of affairs in the island. Only those who paid twenty-five pesos direct contribution had the right of suffrage. The press remained subject to previous censorship, its principal function being to swing the incense-burner; the right of public reunion was unknown, and if known would have been impracticable; the majority of the respectable citizens lived under constant apprehension lest they should be secretly accused of disloyalty and prosecuted. Rumors of conspiracies, filibustering expeditions, clandestine introductions of arms, and attempts at insurrection were the order of the day. Every Liberal was sure to be inscribed on the lists of "suspects," harassed and persecuted.

A seditious movement among the garrison on the 7th of June, 1867, gave Governor Marchessi a pretext for banishing about a dozen of the leading inhabitants of the capital, an arbitrary proceeding which was afterward disapproved by the Government in Madrid.

Such a situation naturally affected the economic conditions of the island. Confidence there was none. Credit was refused. Capital emigrated with its possessors. Commerce and agriculture languished. Misery spread over the land. The treasury was empty, for no contributions could be collected from an impoverished population, and the island's future was compromised by loans at usurious rates.

The dethronement of Isabel II, and the revolution of September, 1868, brought a change for the better. The injustice done to the Antilles by the Cortes of 1873 was repaired, and the island was again called upon to elect representatives. The first meetings with that object were held in February, 1869.

The ideas and tendencies of the Liberal and Conservative parties among the native Puerto Ricans were now beginning to be defined. Each party had its organ in the press[56] and advocated its principles; the authorities stood aloof; the elections came off in an orderly manner (May, 1869); the Conservatives carried the first and third districts, the Liberals the second.

It may be said that the political education of the Puerto Ricans commenced with the royal decree of 1865, which authorized the minister of ultramarine

78

affairs, Canovas del Castillo, to draw up a report from the information to be furnished by special commissioners to be elected in Puerto Rico and Cuba, which information was to serve as a basis for the enactment of special laws for the government of each island. This gave the commissioners an opportunity to discuss their views on insular government with the leading public men of Spain, and they profited by these discussions till 1867, when they returned.

The question of the abolition of slavery had not been brought to a decision. The insular deputies were almost equally divided in their opinions for and against, but the revolutionary committee in its manifesto declared that from September 19, 1868, all children born of a slave mother should be free.

In Puerto Rico this measure remained without effect owing to the arbitrary and reactionist character of the governor who was appointed to succeed Don Julian Pavia, during whose just and prudent administration the so-called Insurrection of Lares happened. It was originally planned by an ex-commissioner to Cortes, Don Ruiz Belviz, and his friend Betánces, who had incurred the resentment of Governor Marchessi, and who were banished in consequence. They obtained the remission of their sentences in Madrid. Betánces returned to Santo Domingo and Belviz started on a tour through Spanish-American republics to solicit assistance in his secessionist plan; but he died in Valparaiso, and Betánces was left to carry it out alone.

September 20, 1868, two or three hundred individuals of all classes and colors, many of them negro slaves brought along by their masters under promise of liberation, met at the coffee plantation of a Mr. Bruckman, an American, who provided them with knives and machetes, of which he had a large stock in readiness. Thus armed they proceeded to the plantation of a Mr. Rosas, who saluted them as "the army of liberators," and announced himself as their general-in-chief, in token whereof he was dressed in the uniform of an American fireman, with a tri-colored scarf across his breast, a flaming sash around his waist, with sword, revolver, and cavalry boots. During the day detachments of men from different parts of the district joined the party and brought the numbers to from eight to ten hundred. The commissariat, not yet being organized, the general-in-chief generously provided an abundant meal for his men, which, washed down with copious drafts of rum, put them in excellent condition to undertake the march on Lares that same evening.

At midnight the peaceful inhabitants of that small town, which lies nestled among precipitous mountains in the interior, were startled from their sleep by loud yells and cries of "Long live Puerto Rico independent! Down with Spain! Death to the Spaniards!" The alcalde and his secretary, who came out in the street to see what the noise was about, were made prisoners and placed in the stocks, where they were soon joined by a number of Spaniards who lived in the town.

The contents of two or three wine and provision shops (pulperias) that were plundered kept the "enthusiasm" alive.

The next day the Republic of Boriquén was proclaimed. To give solemnity to the occasion, the curate was forced to hold a thanksgiving service and sing a Te Deum, after which the Provisional Government was installed. Francisco Ramirez, a small landholder, was the president. The justice of the peace was made secretary of government, his clerk became secretary of finance, another clerk was made secretary of justice, and the lessee of a cockpit secretary of state. The "alcaldia" was the executive's palace, and the queen's portrait, which hung in the room, was replaced by a white flag with the inscription: "Long live free Puerto Rico! Liberty or Death! 1868."

The declaration of independence came next. All Spaniards were ordered to leave the island with their families within three days, failing which they would be considered as citizens of the new-born republic and obliged to take arms in its defense; in case of refusal they would be treated as traitors.

The next important step was to form a plan of campaign. It was agreed to divide "the army" in two columns and march them the following day on the towns of Pepino and Camuy; but when morning came it appeared that the night air had cooled the enthusiasm of more than half the number of "liberators," and that, considering discretion the better part of valor, they had returned to their homes.

However, there were about three hundred men left, and with these the "commander-in-chief" marched upon Pepino. When the inhabitants became aware of the approach of their liberators they ran to shut themselves up in their houses. The column made a short halt at a "pulperia" in the outskirts of the town, to take some "refreshment," and then boldly penetrated to the plaza, where it was met by sixteen loyal militiamen. A number of shots were exchanged. One "libertador" was killed and two or three wounded, when suddenly some one cried: "The soldiers are coming!" This was the signal for a general *sauve qui peut*, and soon Commander Rojas with a few of his "officers" were left alone. It is said that he tried to rally his panic-stricken warriors, but they would not listen to him. Then he returned to his plantation a sadder, but, presumably, a wiser man.[57]

As soon as the news of the disturbance reached San Juan, the Governor sent Lieutenant-Colonel Gamar in pursuit of the rebels, with orders to investigate the details of the movement and make a list of names of all those implicated. Rosas and all his followers were taken prisoners without resistance. Bruckman and a Venezuelan resisted and were shot down.

Here was an opportunity for the reactionists to visit on the heads of all the members of the reform party the offense of a few misguided jíbaros, and they tried hard to persuade the governor to adopt severe measures against their enemies; but General Pavia was a just and a prudent man, and he placed the rebels at the disposition of the civil court. They were imprisoned in Lares, Arecibo, and Aguadilla, and, while awaiting their trial, an epidemic, brought on by the unsanitary conditions of the prisons in which they were packed, speedily carried off seventy-nine of them.

Of the rest seven were condemned to death, but the governor pardoned five. The remaining two were pardoned by his successor.

So ended the insurrection of Lares. During the trial of the rebels, the same members of the reform party who had been banished by Governor Marchessi, Don Julian Blanco, Don José Julian Acosta, Don Pedro Goico, Don Rufino Goenaga, and Don Calixto Romero, were denounced as the leaders of the

80

Separatist movement. They were imprisoned, but were soon after found to have been falsely accused and liberated.

Until the arrival of General Don Gabriel Baldrich as governor (May, 1870), Puerto Rico benefited little by the revolution of September, 1868. The insurrection in Cuba, which coincided with the movement in Lares, made Sanz, the successor of Pavia, a man of arbitrary character and reactionary principles, adopt a policy more suspicious and intransigent than ever (from 1869 to 1870), but Governor Baldrich was a staunch Liberal, and the Separatist phantom which had haunted his predecessor had no terrors for him. From the day of his arrival, the dense atmosphere of obstruction, distrust, and jealousy in which the island was suffocating cleared. The rumors of conspiracies ceased, political opinions were respected, the Liberals could publicly express their desire for reform without being subjected to insult and persecution. The gag was removed from the mouth of the press and each party had its proper organ. The municipal elections came off peaceably, and the Provincial Deputation, composed entirely of Liberal reformists, was inaugurated April 1, 1871.

General Baldrich was terribly harassed by the intransigents here and in the Peninsula. He was accused of being an enemy of Spain and of protecting the Separatists. Meetings were held denouncing his administration, menaces of expulsion were uttered, and he was insulted even in his own palace. Violent opposition to his reform measures were carried to such an extent that he was at last obliged to declare the capital in a state of siege (July 26, 1871).

On September 27th of the same year he left Puerto Rico disgusted, much to the regret of the enlightened part of the population, which had, for the first time, enjoyed for a short period the benefits of political freedom. As a proof of the disposition of the majority of the people they had elected eighteen Liberal reformists as Deputies to Cortes out of the nineteen that corresponded to the island.

Baldrich's successor was General Ramon Gomez Pulido, nicknamed "coco seco" (dried coconut) on account of his shriveled appearance. Although appointed by a Radical Ministry, he inaugurated a reactionary policy. He ordered new elections to be held at once, and soon filled the prisons of the island with Liberal reformists. He was followed by General Don Simon de la Torre (1872). His reform measures met with still fiercer opposition than that which General Baldrich encountered. He also was forced to declare the state of siege in the capital and landed the marines of a Spanish war-ship that happened to be in the port. He posted them in the Morro and San Cristobal forts, with the guns pointed on the city, threatening to bombard it if the "inconditionals" who had tried to suborn the garrison carried their intention of promoting an insurrection into effect. He removed the chief of the staff from his post and sent him to Spain, relieved the colonel of the Puerto Rican battalion and the two colonels in Mayaguez and Ponce from their respective commands, and maintained order with a strong hand till he was recalled by the Government in Madrid through the machinations of his opponents.

During the interval between the departure of General Baldrich and the arrival in

April, 1873, of Lieutenant-General Primo de Rivero, there happened what was called "the insurrection of Camuy," in which three men were killed, two wounded, and sixteen taken prisoners, which turned out to have been an unwarrantable aggression on the part of the reactionists, falsely reported as an attempt at insurrection.

General Primo de Rivero brought with him the proclamation of the abolition of slavery and Article I of the Constitution of 1869, whereby the inhabitants of the island were recognized as Spaniards.

Great popular rejoicings followed these proclamations. In San Juan processions paraded the streets amid "vivas" to Spain, to the Republic, and to Liberty. In Ponce the people and the soldiers fraternized, and the long-cherished aspirations of the inhabitants seemed to be realized at last.

But they were soon to be undeceived. The Republican authorities in the metropolis sent Sanz, the reactionist, as governor for the second time. His first act was to suspend the individual guarantees granted by the Constitution, then he abolished the Provincial Deputation, dissolved the municipalities in which the Liberal reformists had a majority, and a new period of persecution set in, in which teachers, clergymen, lawyers, and judges—in short, all who were distinguished by superior education and their liberal ideas—were punished for the crime of having striven with deed or tongue or pen for the progress and welfare of the land of their birth.

FOOTNOTES:

[Footnote 53: Estudio Historico. San Juan, 1899.]

[Footnote 54: Cards, rum, and women.]

[Footnote 55: He had been President of the Royal Academy.]

[Footnote 56: El Porvenir, for the Liberals, the Boletin Mercantíl, for the Conservatives.]

[Footnote 57: Extracts from the History of the Insurrection of Lares, by José Perez Moris.]

CHAPTER XXVI
GENERAL CONDITIONS OF THE ISLAND—THE DAWN OF FREEDOM
1874-1898

The Spanish Republic was but short lived. From the day of its proclamation (February 11, 1873) to the landing in Barcelona of Alphonso XII in the early days of 1876 its history is the record of an uninterrupted series of popular tumults.

The political restlessness in the Peninsula, accentuating as it did the party antagonisms in Cuba and Puerto Rico, led the governors, most of whom were chosen for their adherence to conservative principles, to endeavor, but in vain, to stem the tide of revolutionary and Separatist ideas with more and more drastic measures of repression.

This persistence of the colonial authorities in the maintenance of an obsolete system of administration, in the face of a universal recognition of the principles of liberty and self-government, added to the immediate effect on the economic and social conditions in this island of the abolition of slavery, for which it was unprepared,[58] brought it once more to the brink of ruin.

From 1873 to 1880 the resources of the island grew gradually less, the country's capital was being consumed without profit, credit became depressed, the best business forecasts turned out illusive, the most intelligent industrial efforts remained sterile. The sun of prosperity which rose over the island in 1815 set again in gloom during this period of seven years.

The causes were clear to every unbiased mind and must have been so even to the prejudiced officials of the Government. They consisted in the anomalous restrictions on the coasting trade, the unjustifiable difference in the duties on Spanish and island produce, the high duty on flour from the United States, the export duties, the extravagant expenditure in the administration, irritating monopolies, and countless abuses, vexatious formalities, and ruinous exactions.

Mr. James McCormick, an intelligent Scotchman, for many years a resident of the island, who, in 1880, was commissioned by the Provincial Deputation to draw up a report on the causes of the agricultural depression in this island and its removal by the introduction of the system of central sugar factories, describes the situation as follows:

" ... The truth is, that the country is in a pitiable condition. Throughout its extent it resents the many drains upon its vitality. Its strength is wasted, and the activities that utilized its favorable natural conditions are paralyzed. The damages sustained have been enormous and it is scarcely possible to appraise them at their true value. With the produce of the soil diminished and the sale thereof at losing prices the value of real estate throughout the island has decreased in alarming proportions. Everybody's resources have been wasted and spent uselessly, and many landholders, wealthy but yesterday, have been ruined if not reduced to misery. The leading merchants and proprietors, men who were identified with the progress of the country and had vast resources at their command, after a long and tenacious struggle have succumbed at last under the accumulation of misfortunes banded against them."

Such was the situation in 1880.

To relieve the financial distress of the country a series of ordinances were enacted[59] which culminated in the reform laws of March 15, 1895, and if royal decrees had had power to cure the incurable or remove the causes that for four centuries had undermined the foundations of Spain's colonial empire, they might, possibly, have sustained the crumbling edifice for some time longer.

But they came too late. The Antilles were slipping from Spain's grasp; nor could Weyler's inhuman proceedings in Cuba nor the tardy concession of a pseudo-autonomy to Puerto Rico arrest the movement.

The laws of March 15, 1895, for the administrative reorganization of Cuba and Puerto Rico, the basis of which was approved by a unanimous vote of the leaders of the Peninsula and Antillean parties in Cortes, remained without application in Cuba because of the insurrection, and in Puerto Rico because of the influence upon the inhabitants of this island of the events in the neighboring island.

After the death of Macéo and of Marti, the two most influential leaders of the

83

revolution, and the terrible measures for suppressing the revolt adopted by Weyler, the Spanish Colonial Minister, Don Tomas Castellano y Villaroya, addressed the Queen Regent December 31, 1896. He declared his belief in the proximate pacification of Cuba, and said: That the moment had arrived for the Government to show to the world (*vide licet* United States) its firm resolution to comply with the spontaneous promises made by the nation by introducing and amplifying in Puerto Rico the reforms in civil government and administration which had been voted by Cortes.

He further stated that the inconditional party in Puerto Rico, guided by the patriotism which distinguished it, showed its complete conformity with the reforms proposed by the Government, and that the "autonomist" party, which, in the beginning, looked upon the proposed reforms with indifference, had also accepted and declared its conformity with them.

Therefore, the minister continued: "It would not be just in the Government to indefinitely postpone the application in Puerto Rico of a law which awakens so many hopes of a better future."

The minister assures the Queen Regent that the proposed laws respond to an ample spirit of decentralization, and expresses confidence that, as soon as possible, her Majesty will introduce in Cuba also, not only the reforms intended by the law of March 15th, but will extend to Puerto Rico the promised measures to provide the Antilles *with an exclusively local administration and economic personnel.* "The reform laws," the minister adds, "will be the foundation of the new regimen, but an additional decree, to be laid before the Cortes, will amplify them in such a way that a truly autonomous administration will be established in our Antilles." Then follow the proposed laws, which are to apply, explain, and complement in Puerto Rico, the reform laws of March 15th—namely, the Provincial law, the Municipal law, and the Electoral law.

The Peninsular electoral law of June, 1890, was adapted to Cuba and Puerto Rico at the suggestion of Sagasta, who, in the exposition to the Queen Regent, which accompanied the project of autonomy, stated: That the inhabitants of the Antilles frequently complained of, and lamented the irritating inequalities which alone were enough to obstruct or entirely prevent the exercise of constitutional privileges, and he concludes with these remarkable words: " … So that, if by arbitrary dispositions without appeal, by penalties imposed by proclamations of the governors-general, or by simply ignoring the laws of procedure, the citizen may be restrained, harassed, deported even to distant territories, it is impossible for him to exercise the right of free speech, free thought, or free writing, or the freedom of instruction, or religious tolerance, nor can he practise the right of union and association." These words constitute a synopsis of the causes that made the Spanish Government's tardy attempts at reform in the administration of its ultramarine possessions illusive; that mocked the people's legitimate aspirations, destroyed their confidence in the promises of the home Government, and made the people of Puerto Rico look upon the American soldiers, when they landed, not as men in search of conquest and spoliation, but as the representatives of a nation enjoying a full measure of the liberties and privileges, for a moderate share of which they had vainly petitioned the mother country through long years of unquestioning loyalty.

The royal decree conceding autonomy to Puerto Rico was signed on November 25, 1897. On April 21, 1898, Governor-General Manuel Macias, suspended the constitutional guarantees and declared the island in state of war. A few months later Puerto Rico, recognized too late as ripe for self-government by the mother country, became a part of the territory of the United States.

FOOTNOTES:

[Footnote 58: The slaveholders were paid in Government bonds (schedules), redeemable in ten years. They lost their labor supply, and had neither capital nor other means to replace it. Their ruin became inevitable. An English or German syndicate bought up the bonds at 15 per cent.]

[Footnote 59: See Part II, chapter on Finances.]

PART II
THE PEOPLE AND THEIR INSTITUTIONS
CHAPTER XXVII
SITUATION AND GENERAL APPEARANCE OF PUERTO RICO

The island of Puerto Rico, situated in the Atlantic Ocean, is about 1,420 miles from New York, 1,000 miles from Havana, 1,050 miles from Key West, 1,200 miles from Panama, 3,450 miles from Land's End in England, and 3,180 from the port of Cadiz. It is about 104 miles in length from east to west, by 34 miles in average breadth, and has an area of 2,970 square miles. It lies eastward of the other greater Antilles, Cuba, Haiti, and Jamaica, and although inferior even to the last of these islands in population and extent, it yields to none of them in fertility.

By its geographical position Puerto Rico is peculiarly adapted to become the center of an extensive commerce. It lies to the windward of Cuba, Santo Domingo, and Jamaica, and of the Gulf of Mexico and Bay of Honduras. It is contiguous to all the English and French Windward Islands, only a few hours distant from the former Danish islands Saint Thomas, Saint John, and Santa Cruz, and a few days' sail from the coast of Venezuela.

Puerto Rico is the fourth in size of the greater Antilles. Its first appearance to the eye of the stranger is striking and picturesque. Nature here offers herself to his contemplation clothed in the splendid vesture of tropical vegetation. The chain of mountains which intersects the island from east to west seems at first sight to form two distinct chains parallel to each other, but closer observation makes it evident that they are in reality corresponding parts of the same chain, with upland valleys and tablelands in the center, which again rise gradually and incorporate themselves with the higher ridges. The height of these mountains is lofty, if compared with those of the other Antilles. The loftiest part is that of Luguillo, or Loquillo, at the northeast extremity of the island, which measures 1,334 Castilian yards, and the highest point, denominated El Yunque, can be seen at the distance of 68 miles at sea. The summit of this ridge is almost always enveloped in mist, and when its sides are overhung by white fleecy clouds it is the certain precursor of the heavy showers which fertilize the northern coast. The soil in the center of the mountains is excellent, and the mountains themselves are susceptible of cultivation to their summits. Several towns and villages are situated among these mountains, where the inhabitants enjoy the coolness of a European spring and a pure and salubrious atmosphere. The town of Albonito, built on a table-land about eight leagues from Ponce, on the southern coast, enjoys a delightful climate.

To the north and south of this interior ridge of mountains, stretching along the seacoasts, are the fertile valleys which produce the chief wealth of the island. From the principal chain smaller ridges run north and south, forming between them innumerable valleys, fertilized by limpid streams which, descending from the mountains, empty themselves into the sea on either coast. In these valleys the majestic beauty of the palm-trees, the pleasant alternation of hill and dale, the lively verdure of the hills, compared with the deeper tints of the forest, the orange trees, especially when covered with their golden fruit, the rivers winding through the dales, the luxuriant fields of sugar-cane, corn, and rice, with here and there a house peeping through a grove of plantains, and cattle grazing in the green pasture, form altogether a landscape of rural beauty scarcely to be surpassed in any country in the world.

The valleys of the north and east coasts are richest in cattle and most picturesque. The pasturage there is always verdant and luxuriant, while those of the south coast, richer in sugar, are often parched by excessive drought, which, however, does not affect their fertility, for water is found near the surface. This same alternation of rain and drought on the north and south coasts is generally observed in all the West India islands.

Few islands of the extent of Puerto Rico are watered by so many streams. Seventeen rivers, taking their rise in the mountains, cross the valleys of the north coast and fall into the sea. Some of these are navigable for two or three leagues from their mouths for small craft. Those of Manati, Loisa, Trabajo, and Arecibo are very deep and broad, and it is difficult to imagine how such large bodies of water can be collected in so short a course. Owing to the heavy surf which continually breaks on the north coast, these rivers have bars across their embouchures which do not allow large vessels to enter. The rivers of Bayamón and Rio Piedras flow into the harbor of the capital, and are also navigable for boats. At Arecibo, at high water, small brigs may enter with perfect safety, notwithstanding the bar. The south, west, and east coasts are also well supplied with water.

From the Cabeza de San Juan, which is the northeast extremity of the island, to Cape Mala Pascua, which lies to the southeast, nine rivers fall into the sea. From Cape Mala Pascua to Point Aguila, which forms the southwest angle of the island, sixteen rivers discharge their waters on the south coast.

On the west coast, three rivers, five rivulets, and several fresh-water lakes communicate with the sea. The rivers of the north coast are well stocked with edible fish.

The roads formed in Puerto Rico during the Spanish administration are constructed on a substantial plan, the center being filled with gravel and stones well cemented. Each town made and repaired the roads of its respective district. Many excellent and solid bridges, with stone abutments, existed at the time of the transfer of the island to the American nation.

The whole line of coast of this island is indented with harbors, bays, and creeks where ships of heavy draft may come to anchor. On the north coast, during the months of November, December, and January, when the wind blows sometimes with violence from the east and northeast, the anchorage is dangerous in all the bays and harbors of that coast, except in the port of San Juan.

On the western coast the spacious bay of Aguadilla is formed by Cape Borrigua and Cape San Francisco. When the southeast winds prevail it is *not* a safe anchorage for ships.

Mayaguez is also an open roadstead on the west coast formed by two projecting capes. It has good anchorage for vessels of large size and is well sheltered from the north winds.

The south coast also abounds in bays and harbors, but those which deserve particular attention are the ports of Guánica and Hobos, or Jovos, near Guayama. In Guánica vessels drawing 21 feet of water may enter with perfect safety and anchor close to the shore. Hobos or Jovos is a haven of considerable importance; sailing vessels of the largest class may anchor and ride in safety; it has 4 fathoms of water in the shallowest part of the entrance, but it is difficult to enter from June to November as the sea breaks with violence at the entrance on account of the southerly winds which prevail at this season.

All the large islands in the tropics enjoy approximately the same climate. The heat, the rains, the seasons, are, with trifling variations, the same in all, but the number of mountains and running streams, the absence of stagnant waters and general cultivation of the land in Puerto Rico do, probably, powerfully contribute to purify the atmosphere and render it more salubrious to Europeans than it otherwise would be. In the mountains one enjoys the coolness of spring, but the valleys, were it not for the daily breeze which blows from the northeast and east, would be almost uninhabitable for white men during part of the year. The climate of the north and south coasts of this island, though under the same tropical influence, is nevertheless essentially different. On the north coast it sometimes rains almost the whole year, while on the south coast sometimes no rain falls for twelve or fourteen months. On the whole, Puerto Rico is one of the healthiest islands in the West Indies, nor is it infested to the same extent as other islands by poisonous snakes and other noxious reptiles. The laborer may sleep in peace and security in the midst of the forest, by the side of the river, or in the meadow with his cattle with no other fear than that of an occasional centipede or guabuá (large hairy spider).

Unlike most tropical islands there are no indigenous quadrupeds and scarcely any of the feathered tribe in the forests. On the rivers there are a few water-fowl and in the forests the green parrot. There are neither monkeys nor rabbits, but rats and mongooses infest the country and sometimes commit dreadful ravages in the sugar-cane. Ants of different species also abound.

CHAPTER XXVIII
ORIGIN, CHARACTER, AND CUSTOMS OF THE PRIMITIVE INHABITANTS OF BORIQUÉN

The origin of the primitive inhabitants of the West Indian Archipelago has been the subject of much learned controversy, ending, like all such discussions, in different theories and more or less verisimilar conjecture.

It appears that at the time of the discovery these islands were inhabited by three races of different origin. One of these races occupied the Bahamas. Columbus describes them as simple, generous, peaceful creatures, whose only weapon was a pointed stick or cane. They were of a light copper color, well-proportioned but slender, rather good-looking, with aquiline noses, salient cheek-bones, medium-sized mouths, long coarse hair. They had, perhaps, formerly occupied the eastern part of the archipelago, whence they had gradually disappeared, driven or exterminated by the Caribs, Caribós, or Guáribos, a savage, warlike, and cruel race, which had invaded the West Indies from the continent by way of the Orinoco, along the tributaries of which river tribes of the same race are still to be found. The larger Antilles, Cuba, Santo Domingo, and Puerto Rico, were occupied by a race which probably originated from some part of the southern division of the northern continent. The chroniclers mention the Guaycures and others as their possible ancestors, and Stahl traces their origin to a mixture of the Phoenicians with the aborigines of remote antiquity.

The information which we possess with regard to the habits and customs of the inhabitants of Boriquén at the time of discovery is too scanty and too unreliable to permit us to form more than a speculative opinion of the degree of culture attained by them.

Friar Abbad, in the fourth chapter of his history, gives us a description of the character and customs of the people of Boriquén taken wholly from the works of Oviedo, Herrera, Robertson, Raynal, and others.

Like most of the aboriginal inhabitants of America, the natives of Boriquén were copper-colored, but somewhat darker than the inhabitants of the neighboring islands. They were shorter of stature than the Spaniards, but corpulent and well-proportioned, with flat noses, wide nostrils, dull eyes, bad teeth, narrow foreheads, the skull artificially flattened before and behind so as to give it a conical shape, with long, black, coarse hair, beardless and hairless on the rest of the body. Says Oviedo: " ... Their heads were not like other people's, their skulls were so hard and thick that the Christians by fighting with them have learned not to strike them on the head because the swords break."

Their whole appearance betrayed a lazy, indolent habit, and they showed extreme aversion to labor or fatigue of any kind. They put forth no exertion save what was necessary to obtain food, and only rose from their "hamácas" or "jamácas," or shook off their habitual indolence to play a game of ball (batey) or attend the dances (areytos) which were accompanied by rude music and the chanting of whatever happened to occupy their minds at the time.

Notwithstanding their indolence and the unsubstantial nature of their food, they were comparatively strong and robust, as they proved in many a personal tussle with the Spaniards.

Clothing was almost unknown. Only the women of mature age used an apron of varying length, the rest, without distinction of age or sex, were naked. They took great pains in painting their bodies with all sorts of grotesque figures, the earthy coloring matter being laid on by means of oily or resinous substances extracted from plants or trees.

These coats of paint, when fresh, served as holiday attire, and protected them from the bites of mosquitoes and other insects. The dandies among them added to this airy apparel a few bright feathers in their hair, a shell or two in their ears and nostrils. And the caciques wore a disk of gold (guarim) the size of a large medal round their necks to denote their rank.

The huts were built square or oblong, raised somewhat above the ground, with only one opening for entrance and exit, cane being the principal building material. The chief piece of furniture was the "hamáca," made with creepers or strips of bark of the "emajágua" tree. The "totúmo" or "jigüera" furnished them with their domestic utensils, as it furnishes the "jíbaro" of to-day with his cups and jugs and basins. Their mode of making fire was the universal one practised by savages. Their arms were the usual macána and bow and arrows, but they did not poison the arrows as did the Caribs. The largest of their canoes, or "piráguas," could contain from 40 to 50 men, and served for purposes of war, but the majority of their canoes were of small size used in navigating the coast and rivers.

There being no mammals in the island, they knew not the use of flesh for food, but they had abundance of fish, and they ate besides whatever creeping or crawling thing they happened to find. These with the yucca from which they made their casabe or bread, maize, yams, and other edible roots, constituted their food supply.

There were in Boriquén, as there are among all primitive races, certain individuals, the embryos of future church functionaries, who were medicine-man, priest, prophet, and general director of the moral and intellectual affairs of the benighted masses, but that is all we know of them.[60]

FOOTNOTES:

[Footnote 60: For further information on this subject, see Estudios Ethnologicos sobre los indios Boriqueños, by A. Stahl, 1888. Revista Puertoriqueña, Año II, tomo II.]

CHAPTER XXIX
THE "JÍBARO," OR PUERTO RICAN PEASANT

"There is in this island a class of inhabitants, not the least numerous by any means, who dwell in swamps and marshes, live on vegetables, and drink muddy water." So wrote Dr. Richard Rey[61] a couple of decades ago, and, although, under the changed political and social conditions, these people, as a class, will soon disappear, they are quite numerous still, and being the product of the peculiar social and political conditions of a past era deserve to be known.

To this considerable part of the population of Puerto Rico the name of "jíbaros" is applied; they are the descendants of the settlers who in the early days of the colonization of the island spread through the interior, and with the assistance of an Indian or negro slave or two cleared and cultivated a piece of land in some isolated locality, where they continued to live from day to day without troubling themselves about the future or about what passed in the rest of the universe.

The modern jíbaro builds his "bohío," or hut, in any place without regard to hygienic conditions, and in its construction follows the same plan and uses the same materials employed in their day by the aboriginal inhabitants. This "bohío" is square or oblong in form, raised on posts two or three feet from the ground, and the materials are cane, the trunks of the coco-palm, entire or cut into boards, and the bark of another species of palm, the "yaguas," which serves for roofing and walls. The interior of these huts is sometimes divided by a partition of reeds into two apartments, in one of which the family sit by day. The other is the sleeping room, where the father, mother, and children, male and female, of all ages, sleep, promiscuously huddled together on a platform of boards or bar bacao.

The majority of the jíbaros are whites. Mestizoes, mulattos, and negroes are numerous also. But we are here concerned with the jíbaro of European descent only, whose redemption from a degraded condition of existence it is to the country's interest should be specially attended to.

Mr. Francisco del Valle Atilés, one of Puerto Rico's distinguished literary men, has left us a circumstantial description of the character and conditions of these rustics.[62] He divides them into three groups: those living in the neighborhood of the large sugar and coffee estates, who earn their living working as peons; the second group comprises the small proprietors who cultivate their own patch of land, and the third, the comparatively well-to-do individuals or small proprietors who usually prefer to live as far as possible from the centers of population.

The jíbaro, as a rule, is well formed, slender, of a delicate constitution, slow in his movements, taciturn, and of a sickly aspect. Occasionally, in the mountainous districts, one meets a man of advanced age still strong and robust doing daily work and mounting on horseback without effort. Such a one will generally be found to be of pure Spanish descent, and to have a numerous family of healthy, good-looking children, but the appearance of the average jíbaro is as described. He looks sickly and anemic in consequence of the insufficient quantity and innutritious quality of the food on which he subsists and the unhealthy conditions of his surroundings. Rice, plantains, sweet potatoes, maize, yams, beans, and salted fish constitute his diet year in year out, and although there are Indian races who could thrive perhaps on such frugal fare, the effect of such a *régime* on individuals of the white race is loss of muscular energy and a consequent craving for stimulants.

His clothing, too, is scanty. He wears no shoes, and when drenched with rain or perspiration he will probably let his garments dry on his body. For the empty feeling in his stomach, the damp and the cold to which he is thus daily exposed, his antidotes are tobacco and rum, the first he chews and smokes. In the use of the second he seldom goes to the extent of intoxication.

Under these conditions, and considering his absolute ignorance and consequent

90

neglect of the laws of hygiene, it is but natural that the Puerto Rican peasant should be subject to the ravages of paludal fever, one of the most dangerous of the endemic diseases of the tropics.

Friar Abbad observes: " ... No cure has yet been discovered (1781) for the intermittent fevers which are often from four to six years in duration. Those who happen to get rid of them recover very slowly; many remain weak and attenuated; the want of nutritious food and the climate conduce to one disease or another, so that those who escape the fever generally die of dropsy."

However, the at first sight apathetic and weak jíbaro, when roused to exertion or when stimulated by personal interest or passion, can display remarkable powers of endurance. Notwithstanding his reputation of being lazy, he will work ten or eleven hours a day if fairly remunerated. Under the Spanish *régime*, when he was forced to present himself on the plantations to work for a few cents from sunrise to sundown, he was slow; or if he was of the small proprietor class, he had to pay an enormous municipal tax on his scanty produce, so that it is very likely that he may often have preferred swinging in his hammock to laboring in the fields for the benefit of the municipal treasury.

Mr. Atilés refers to the premature awakening among the rustic population of this island of the procreative instincts, and the consequent increase in their numbers notwithstanding the high rate of mortality. The fecundity of the women is notable; from six to ten children in a family seems to be the normal number.

Intellectually the jíbaro is as poor as he is physically. His illiteracy is complete; his speech is notoriously incorrect; his songs, if not of a silly, meaningless character, are often obscene; sometimes they betray the existence of a poetic sentiment. These songs are usually accompanied by the music of a stringed instrument of the guitar kind made by the musician himself, to which is added the "güiro," a kind of ribbed gourd which is scraped with a small stick to the measure of the tune, and produces a noise very trying to the nerves of a person not accustomed to it.

In religion the jíbaro professes Catholicism with a large admixture of fetichism. His moral sense is blunt in many respects.

Colonel Flinter[63] gives the following description of the jíbaros of his day, which also applies to them to-day:

"They are very civil in their manners, but, though they seem all simplicity and humility, they are so acute in their dealings that they are sure to deceive a person who is not very guarded. Although they would scorn to commit a robbery, yet they think it only fair to deceive or overreach in a bargain. Like the peasantry of Ireland, they are proverbial for their hospitality, and, like them, they are ever ready to fight on the slightest provocation. They swing themselves to and fro in their hammocks all day long, smoking their cigars or scraping a guitar. The plantain grove which surrounds their houses, and the coffee tree which grows almost without cultivation, afford them a frugal subsistence. If with these they have a cow and a horse, they consider themselves rich and happy. Happy indeed they are; they feel neither the pangs nor remorse which follow the steps of disappointed ambition nor the daily wants experienced by the poor inhabitants of northern regions."

This entirely materialistic conception of happiness which, it is certain, the Puerto Rican peasant still entertains, is now giving way slowly but surely before the new influences that are being brought to bear on himself and on his surroundings. The touch of education is dispelling the darkness of ignorance that enveloped the rural districts of this island until lately; industrial activity is placing the means of greater comfort within the reach of every one who cares to work for them; the observance of the laws of health is beginning to be enforced, even in the bohío, and with them will come a greater morality. In a word, in ten years the Puerto Rican jíbaro will have disappeared, and in his place there will be an industrious, well-behaved, and no longer illiterate class of field laborers, with a nobler conception of happiness than that to which they have aspired for many generations.

FOOTNOTES:

[Footnote 61: Estudio sobre el paludismo en Puerto Rico.]

[Footnote 62: El campesino Puertoriqueño, sus condiciones, etc. Revista Puertoriqueña, vols. ii, iii, 1887, 1888.]

[Footnote 63: An Account of the Present State of the Island of Puerto Rico. London, 1834.]

CHAPTER XXX
ORIGIN AND CHARACTER OF THE MODERN INHABITANTS OF PUERTO RICO

During the initial period of conquest and colonization, no Spanish females came to this or any other of the conquered territories. Soldiers, mariners, monks, and adventurers brought no families with them; so that by the side of the aboriginals and the Spaniards "pur sang" there sprang up an indigenous population of mestizos.

The result of the union of two physically, ethically, and intellectually widely differing races is *not* the transmission to the progeny of any or all of the superior qualities of the progenitor, but rather his own moral degradation. The mestizos of Spanish America, the Eurasians of the East Indies, the mulattoes of Africa are moral, as well as physical hybrids in whose character, as a rule, the worst qualities of the two races from which they spring predominate. It is only in subsequent generations, after oft-repeated crossings and recrossings, that atavism takes place, or that the fusion of the two races is finally consummated through the preponderance of the physiological attributes of the ancestor of superior race.

The early introduction of negro slaves, almost exclusively males, the affinity between them and the Indians, the state of common servitude and close, daily contact produced another race. By the side of the mestizo there grew up the zambo. Later, when negro women were brought from Santo Domingo or other islands, the mulatto was added.

Considering the class to which the majority of the first Spanish settlers in this island belonged, the social status resulting from these additions to their number could be but little superior to that of the aboriginals themselves.

The necessity of raising that status by the introduction of white married couples was manifest to the king's officers in the island, who asked the Government in 1534 to send them 50 such couples. It was not done. Fifty bachelors came instead, whose arrival lowered the moral standard still further.

It was late in the island's history before the influx of respectable foreigners and their families began to diffuse a higher ethical tone among the creoles of the better class. Unfortunately, the daily contact of the lower and middle classes with the soldiers of the garrison did not tend to improve their character and manners, and the effects of this contact are clearly traceable to-day in the manners and language of the common people.

From the crossings in the first degree of the Indian, negro, and white races, and their subsequent recrossings, there arose in course of time a mixed race of so many gradations of color that it became difficult in many instances to tell from the outward appearance of an individual to what original stock he belonged; and, it being the established rule in all Spanish colonies to grant no civil or military employment above a certain grade to any but Peninsulars or their descendants of pure blood, it became necessary to demand from every candidate documentary evidence that he had no Indian or negro blood in his veins. This was called presenting an "expediente de sangre," and the practise remained in force till the year 1870, when Marshal Serrano abolished it.

Whether it be due to atavism, or whether, as is more likely, the Indians did not really become extinct till much later than the period at which it is generally supposed their final fusion into the two exotic races took place,[64] it is certain that Indian characteristics, physical and ethical, still largely prevail among the rural population of Puerto Rico, as observed by Schoelzer and other ethnologists.

The evolution of a new type of life is now in course of process. In the meantime, we have Mr. Salvador Brau's authority[65] for stating the general character of the present generation of Puerto Ricans to be made up of the distinctive qualities of the three races from which they are descended, to wit: indolence, taciturnity, sobriety, disinterestedness, hospitality, inherited from their Indian ancestors; physical endurance, sensuality, and fatalism from their negro progenitors; and love of display, love of country, independence, devotion, perseverance, and chivalry from their Spanish sires.

A somewhat sarcastic reference to the characteristics due to the Spanish blood in them was made in 1644 by Bishop Damian de Haro in a letter to a friend, wherein, speaking of his diocesans, he says that they are of very chivalric extraction, for, "he who is not descended from the House of Austria is related to the Dauphin of France or to Charlemagne." He draws an amusing picture of the inhabitants of the capital, saying that at the time there were about 200 males and 4,000 women "between black and mulatto." He complains that there are no grapes in the country; that the melons are red, and that the butcher retails turtle meat instead of beef or pork; yet, says he, "my table is a bishop's table for all that."

To a lady in Santo Domingo he sent the following sonnet:

This is a small island, lady,
With neither money nor provisions;

The blacks go naked as they do yonder,
And there 're more people in the Seville prison.
The Castilian coats of arms
Are conspicuous by their absence,
But there are plenty cavaliers
Who deal in hides and ginger,
There's water in the tanks, when 't rains,
A cathedral, but no priests,
Handsome women, but not elegant,
Greed and envy are indigenous.
Plenty of heat and palm-tree shade,
And best of all a refreshing breeze.

Of the moral defects of the people it would be invidious to speak. The lower classes are not remarkable for their respect for the property of others. On the subject of morality among the rural population we may cite Count de Caspe, the governor's report to the king: " ... Destitute as they are of religious instruction and moral restraint, their unions are without the sanction of religious or civil law, and last just as long as their sensual appetites last; it may therefore be truly said, that in the rural districts of Puerto Rico the family, morally constituted, does not exist."

Colonel Flinter's account of the people and social conditions of Puerto Rico in 1834 is a rather flattering one, though he acknowledges that the island had a bad reputation on account of the lawless character of the lower class of inhabitants.

All this has greatly changed for the better, but much remains to be done in the way of moral improvement.

FOOTNOTES:

[Footnote 64: Abbad points out that in 1710-'20 there were still two Indian settlements in the neighborhood of Añasco and San German.]

[Footnote 65: Puerto Rico y su historia, p. 369.]

CHAPTER XXXI
NEGRO SLAVERY IN PUERTO RICO

From the early days of the conquest the black race appeared side by side with the white race. Both supplanted the native race, and both have marched parallel ever since, sometimes separately, sometimes mixing their blood.

The introduction of African negroes into Puerto Rico made the institution of slavery permanent. It is true that King Ferdinand ordered the reduction to slavery of all rebellious Indians in 1511, but he revoked the order the next year. The negro was and remained a slave. For centuries he had been looked upon as a special creation for the purpose of servitude, and the Spaniards were accustomed to see him daily offered for sale in the markets of Andalusia.

Notwithstanding the practical reduction to slavery of the Indians of la Española by Columbus, under the title of "repartimientos," negro slaves were introduced into that island as early as 1502, when a certain Juan Sanchez and Alfonso Bravo received royal permission to carry five caravels of slaves to the newly discovered island. Ovando, who was governor at the time, protested strongly on the ground that the negroes escaped to the forests and mountains, where they joined the rebellious or fugitive Indians and made their subjugation much more difficult. The same thing happened later in San Juan.

In this island special permission was necessary to introduce negroes. Sedeño and the smelter of ores, Giron, who came here in 1510, made oath that the two slaves each brought with them were for their personal service only. In 1513 their general introduction was authorized by royal schedule on payment of two ducats per head.

Cardinal Cisneros prohibited the export of negro slaves from Spain in 1516; but the efforts of Father Las Casas to alleviate the lot of the Indians by the introduction of what he believed, with the rest of his contemporaries, to be providentially ordained slaves, obtained from Charles II a concession in favor of Garrebod, the king's high steward, to ship 4,000 negroes to la Española, Cuba, Puerto Rico, and Jamaica (1517). Garrebod sold the concession to some merchants of Genoa.

With the same view of saving the Indians, the Jerome fathers, who governed the Antilles in 1518, requested the emperor's permission to fit out slave-ships themselves and send them to the coast of Africa for negroes. It appears that this permission was not granted; but in 1528 another concession to introduce 4,000 negroes into the Antilles was given to some Germans, who, however, did not comply with the terms of the contract.

Negroes were scarce and dear in San Juan at this period, which caused the authorities to petition the emperor for permission to each settler to bring two slaves free of duty, and, this being granted, it gave rise to abuse, as the city officers in their address of thanks to the empress, stated at the same time that many took advantage of the privilege to transfer or sell their permit in Seville without coming to the island. Then it was enacted that slaves should be introduced only by authorized traffickers, who soon raised the price to 60 or 70 Castilian dollars per head. The crown officers in the island protested, and asked that every settler might be permitted to bring 10 or 12 negroes, paying the duty of 2 ducats per head, which had been imposed by King Ferdinand in 1513. A new deposit of gold had been discovered about this time (1533), and the hope that others might be found now induced the colonists to buy the negroes from the authorized traders on credit at very high prices, to be paid with the gold which the slaves should be made instrumental in discovering. But the longed-for metal did not appear. The purchasers could not pay. Many had their property embargoed and sold, and were ruined. Some were imprisoned, others escaped to the mountains or left the island.

From 1536 to 1553 the authorities kept asking for negroes; sometimes offering to pay duty, at others soliciting their free introduction; now complaining that the colonists escaped *with their slaves* to Mexico and Peru, then lamenting that the German merchants, who had the monopoly of the traffic, took them to all the other Antilles, but would bring none to this island. However, 1,500 African slaves entered here at different times during those seventeen years, without reckoning the large numbers that were introduced as contraband.

95

Philip II tried to reduce the exorbitant prices exacted by the German monopolists of the West Indian slave-trade, but, finding that his efforts to do so diminished the importation, he revoked his ordinances.

A Genoese banking-house, having made him large advances to help equip the great Armada for the invasion of England, obtained the next monopoly (1580).

During the course of the seventeenth century the privilege of introducing African slaves into the Antilles was sold successively to Genoese, Portuguese, Holland, French, and Spanish companies. The traffic was an exceedingly profitable one, not so much on account of the high prices obtained for the negroes as on account of the contraband trade in all kinds of merchandise that accompanied it. From 1613 to 1621 during the government of Felipe de Beaumont, 11 ship-loads of slaves entered San Juan harbor.

During the eighteenth century the traffic expanded still more. To induce England to abandon the cause of the House of Austria, for which that nation was fighting, Philip V offered it the exclusive privilege of introducing 140,000 negro slaves into the Spanish-American colonies within a period of thirty years; the monopolists to pay 33-13 silver crowns for each negro introduced, to the Spanish Government.[66]

War interrupted this contract several times, and long before the termination of the thirty years the English ceased to import slaves.

Several contracts for the importation of slaves into the Antilles were made from 1760 to the end of the century. First a contract was made with Miguel Uriarte to take 15,000 slaves to different parts of Spanish America. In 1765 the king sanctioned the introduction by the Carácas company of 2,000 slaves to replace the Indians in Carácas and Maraeaíbo, who had died of smallpox. All duties on the introduction of negroes into Santo Domingo, Cuba, Puerto Rico, Margarita, and Trinidad were commuted in the same year for a moderate capitation tax, and the Spanish firm of Aguirre, Aristegui & Co. was authorized to provide the Antilles with negroes, on condition of reducing the price 10 pesos per head, besides the amount of abolished duty.

This firm abused the privileges granted, and the inhabitants of all the colonies, excepting Peru, Chile, and the Argentina, were allowed to provide themselves, as best they could, with slaves from the French colonies while the war lasted (1780).

Four years later, January 16, 1784, a certain Lenormand, of Xantes, received the king's permission to take a ship-load of African slaves to Puerto Rico on condition of paying 6 per cent of the product to the Government.

In this same year the barbarous custom of branding the slaves was abolished.

The abominable traffic was declared entirely free in Santo Domingo, Cuba, and Puerto Rico by royal decree, February 28, 1789. Foreign ships were placed under certain restrictions, but a bounty of 4 pesos per head was paid for negroes brought in Spanish bottoms, to meet which a per capita tax of 2 pesos per head on domestic slaves was levied.

By this time the famous debates in the British Parliament and other signs of the times announced the dawn of freedom for the oppressed African race. Wilberforce, Clarkson, and Buxton, the English abolitionists, continued their

96

denunciations of the demoralizing institution. Their effects were crowned with success in 1833. The traffic was abolished, and ten years later Great Britain emancipated more than twelve million slaves in her East and West Indian possessions, paying the masters over one hundred millions of dollars as indemnity.

Spain agreed in 1817 to abolish the slave-trade in her dominions by May 30,1820. By Articles 3 and 4 of the convention, England offered to pay to Spain $20,000,000 as complete compensation to his Catholic Majesty's subjects who were engaged in the traffic.

The Spanish Government illegally employed this money to purchase from Russia a fleet of five ships of the line and eight frigates.

The slaves in Puerto Rico were not emancipated until March 22, 1873, when 31,000 were manumitted in one day, at a cost to the Government of 200 pesos each, plus the interest on the bonds that were issued.

The nature of the relations between the master and the slave in Puerto Rico probably did not differ much from that which existed between them in the other Spanish colonies. But these relations began to assume an aspect of distrust and severity on the one hand and sullen resentment on the other when the war of extermination between whites and blacks in Santo Domingo and the establishment of a negro republic in Haiti made it possible for the flame of negro insurrection to be wafted across the narrow space of water that separates the two islands.

There was sufficient ground for such apprehension. The free colored population in Puerto Rico at that time (1830-'34) numbered 127,287, the slaves 34,240, as against 162,311 whites, among whom many were of mixed blood.[67] Prim, the governor-general, to suppress every attempt at insurrection, issued the proclamation, of which the following is a synopsis:

"I, John Prim, Count of Ecus, etc., etc., etc.

"Whereas, The critical circumstances of the times and the afflictive condition of the countries in the neighborhood of this island, some of which are torn by civil war, and others engaged in a war of extermination between the white and black races; it is incumbent on me to dictate efficacious measures to prevent the spread of these calamities to our pacific soil.... I have decreed as follows:

"ARTICLE 1. All offenses committed by individuals of African race, whether free or slaves, shall be judged by court-martial.

"ART. 2. Any individual of African race, whether free or slave, who shall offer armed resistance to a white, shall be shot, if a slave, and have his right hand cut off by the public executioner, if a free man. Should he be wounded he shall be shot.

"ART. 3. If any individual of African race, whether slave or free, shall insult, menace, or maltreat, in any way, a white person, he will be condemned to five years of penal servitude, if a slave, and according to the circumstances of the case, if free.

"ART. 4. The owners of slaves are hereby authorized to correct and chastise them for slight misdemeanors, without any civil or military functionary having the

97

right to interfere.

"ART. 5. If any slave shall rebel against his master, the latter is authorized to kill him on the spot.

"ART. 6 orders the military commanders of the 8 departments of the island to decide all cases of offenses committed by colored people within twenty-four hours of their denunciation."

This Draconic decree is signed, Puerto Rico, May 31, 1843.

FOOTNOTES:

[Footnote 66: Treaty of Madrid, March 16, 1713, ratified by the treaty of Utrecht. There were two kinds of silver crowns, one of 8 pesetas, the other of 10, worth respectively 4 and 5 English shillings.]

[Footnote 67: Flinter, p. 211.]

CHAPTER XXXII
INCREASE OF POPULATION

ALL statements of definite numbers with respect to the aboriginal population of this island are essentially fabulous. Columbus touched at only one port on the western shore. He remained there but a few days and did not come in contact with the inhabitants. Ponce and his men conquered but a part of the island, and had no time to study the question of population, even if they had had the inclination to do so. They did not count the enemy in time of war, and only interested themselves in the number of prisoners which to them constituted the spoils of conquest. Any calculation regarding the numbers that remained at large, based on the number of Indians distributed, can not be correct.

The same may be said of the computations of the population of the island made by Abbad, O'Reilly, and others at a time when there was not a correct statistical survey existing in the most civilized countries of Europe. None of these computations exceed the limits of mere conjecture.

With regard to the attempts to explain the causes of the decay and ultimate disappearance of the aboriginal race, this subject also appears to be involved in considerable doubt and obscurity, notwithstanding the positive statements of native writers regarding it. It has been impossible to ascertain in what degree they became amalgamated by intermarriage with the conquerors; yet, that it has been to a much larger degree than generally supposed, is proved by the fact that many of the inhabitants, classed as white, have, both in their features and manners, definite traces of the Indian race.[68]

With respect to the census taken by the Spanish authorities at different times, though they may have taken great pains to obtain correct statistical accounts, there is little doubt that the real numbers greatly exceeded those which appear in the official returns. The reason for this discrepancy is supposed by the author mentioned to have been the *direct contribution* which was levied on agricultural property, inducing the landed proprietors to conceal the real number of their slaves in order to make their crops appear to have been *smaller* than they were.

Nor does it appear that the increase in the population of Puerto Rico is so much indebted to immigration as is generally supposed; for, notwithstanding the advantages offered to colonists by the Government in 1815, and the influx of settlers from Santo Domingo and Venezuela during the civil wars in these republics, there were only 2,833 naturalized foreigners in the island in 1830. It appears also that the Spanish immigration from the revolted colonies did not exceed 7,000 souls.

Puerto Rico had the reputation of being very poor, consequently, no immigrants were attracted by the prospect of money-making. The increase in the population of this island is sufficiently accounted for by the fact that three-fourths of the inhabitants are engaged in agricultural pursuits, which, of all occupations, are most conducive to health. To which must be added the people's frugal habits, the easy morals, the effect of climate, and the fecundity of the women of all mixed races. These, and the peace which the island enjoyed in the beginning of the nineteenth century, together with the abolition of some of the restrictions on commerce and industry, promoted an era of prosperity the like of which the inhabitants had never before known, and the natural consequence was increase in numbers.

"In those days," says Colonel Flinter, "if some perfect stranger had dropped from the clouds as it were, on this island, naked, without any other auxiliaries than health and strength, he might have married the next day and maintained a family without suffering more hardships or privations than fall to the lot of every laborer in the ordinary process of clearing and cultivating a piece of land."

The earliest information on the subject was given by Alexander O'Reilly, the royal commissioner to the Antilles in 1765, who enumerates a list of 24 towns and settlements with a total population of

Free men, women, and children of all colors....39,846
Slaves of both sexes, including their children 5,037
Total...44,883

Abbad, in his "general statistics of the island," corresponding to the end of the year 1776, gives the details of the population in 30 "partidas," or ecclesiastical districts, as follows:
Whites 29,263
Free colored people 33,808
Free blacks 2,803
Other free people ("agregados") 7,835
Slaves 6,537

Total 80,246

That is to say, an increase of 7-311 per cent per annum during the eleven years elapsed since O'Reilly's computation, which was a period of constant apprehension of attacks by pirates and privateers.

From 1782 to 1802 there were three censuses taken showing the following totals:
In 1782 81,180 souls. " 1792 115,557 " " 1802 163,192 "

From 1800 to 1815, there was universal poverty and depression in the island in consequence of the prohibitive system introduced by the Spanish authorities in all branches of commerce and industry, and the sudden failure of the annual remittances from Mexico in consequence of the insurrection. Still, the population had increased from 163,192 in 1802 to 220,892 in 1815.

From this year forward a great improvement in the island's general condition set in, thanks to the efforts of Don Ramon Power, Puerto Rico's delegate to Cortes, who obtained for the island, in November, 1811, the freedom of commerce with foreign nations, and by the appointment of Intendant Ramirez procured the suppression of many abuses and monopolies.

The royal schedule of August 13, 1815, called "the schedule of graces," also contributed to the general improvement by the opening of the ports to immigrants, though short-sighted restrictions destroyed the beneficent effects of the measure to no small extent. However, immigrants came, and among them 83 practical agriculturists from Louisiana, with slaves and capital.

The census of 1834 gives the total population on an area of 330 square leagues, in the proportion of 981-16 inhabitants per square league, as follows:

Whites......................... 188,869
Colored.........................126,400
Slaves.......................... 41,817
Troops and prisoners............. 1,730
Total......................... 358,836

This year shows an increase in the proportion of the slave population over the free population since 1815, due to the free introduction of slaves and the slaves brought by the immigrants.

A statistical commission for the island of Puerto Rico was created in 1845. The census taken under its auspices in the following year may be considered reliable. The total figures are:

Whites......................... 216,083
Free colored.....................175,791
Slaves.......................... 51,265
Total......................... 443,139

In 1855 cholera morbus raged throughout the island, especially among the colored population, and carried off 9,529 slaves alone.

The next census shows the progressive increase of inhabitants. It was conducted by royal decree of September 30,1858, on the nights of December 25 and 26, 1860. The official memorial gives the following totals:

Whites............................. 300,430
Free colored........................ 341,015
Slaves.............................. 41,736
Unclassified........................ 127
Total........................... 583,308

or 1,802.2 inhabitants per square league; one of the densest populations on the globe, and the densest in the Antilles at the time except Barbados.

The annual increase of population in Puerto Rico, according to the calculations of Colonel Flinter, was:

From 1778-1802 ... 24 years ... 5-12 per cent per annum. " 1802-1812 ... 10 "

100

... 1-15 " " 1812-1820 ... 8 " ... 3-14 " " " 1820-1830 ... 10 " ... 4 " " " 1830-1846 ... 16 " ... 3-15 " " " 1846-1860 ... 14 " ... 3.72 " "

or an average annual increase of a little less than 4 per cent in a period of eighty-two years.

From 1860 to 1864 the increase was small, but from that year to the end of Spanish domination the percentage of increase was larger than in any of the preceding periods.

The treaty of Paris brought 894,302 souls under the protection of the American flag. They consisted of 570,187 whites, 239,808 of mixed race, and 75,824 negroes.

FOOTNOTES:
[Footnote 68: Flinter.]

CHAPTER XXXIII
AGRICULTURE IN PUERTO RICO

After the cessation of the gold produce, when the colonists were forced by necessity to dedicate themselves to agriculture, they met with many adverse conditions:

The incursions of the Caribs, the hurricanes of 1530 and 1537, the emigration to Peru and Mexico, the internal dissensions, and last, but not least, the heavy taxes. The colonists had found the soil of Puerto Rico admirably adapted to sugar-cane, which they brought from Santo Domingo, where Columbus had introduced it on his second voyage, and the nascent sugar industry was beginning to prosper and expand when a royal decree imposing a heavy tax on sugar came to strangle it in its birth. Bishop Bastidas called the Government's attention to the fact in a letter dated March 20, 1544, in which he says: " ... The new tax to be paid on sugar in this island, as ordained by your Majesty, will still further reduce the number of mills, which have been diminishing of late. Let this tax be suspended and the mills in course of construction will be finished, while the erection of others will be encouraged."

The prelate's efforts seem to have produced a favorable effect. Treasurer Castellanos, in 1546, loaned 6,000 pesos for the Government's account, to two colonists for the erection of two sugar-cane mills. In 1548 Gregorio Santolaya built, in the neighborhood of the capital, the first cane-mill turned by water-power, and two mills moved by horse-power. Another water-power mill was mounted in 1549 on the estate of Alonzo Perez Martel with the assistance of 1,500 pesos lent by the king. Loans for the same purpose continued to be made for years after.

But if the Government encouraged the sugar industry with one hand, with the other it checked its development, together with that of other agricultural industries appropriate to the island, by means of prohibitive legislation, monopolies, and other oppressive measures. The effects of this administrative stupidity were still patent a century later. Bishop Fray Lopez de Haro wrote in 1644: " ... The only crop in this island is ginger, and it is so depreciated that nobody buys it or wants to take it to Spain.... There are many cattle farms in the country, and 7 sugar mills, where the families live with their slaves the whole year round."

Canon Torres Vargas, in his Memoirs, amplifies the bishop's statement, stating that the principal articles of commerce of the island were ginger, hides, and sugar, and he gives the location of the above-mentioned 7 sugar-cane mills. The total annual produce of ginger had been as much as 14,000 centals, but, with the war and excessive supply, the price had gone down, and in the year he wrote (1646) only 4,000 centals had been harvested. He informs us, too, that cacáo had been planted in sufficient quantity to send ship-loads to Spain within four years. The number of hides annually exported to Spain was 8,000 to 10,000. Tobacco had begun to be cultivated within the last ten years, and its exportation had commenced. He pronounces it better than the tobacco of Havana, Santo Domingo, and Margarita, but not as good as that of Barinas.

The cultivation of tobacco in Puerto Rico was permitted by a special law in 1614, but the sale of it to foreigners was prohibited *under penalty of death and confiscation of property.*[69] These and other stringent measures dictated in 1777 and 1784 by their very severity defeated their own purpose, and the laws, to a great extent, remained a dead letter.

The cultivation of cacáo in Puerto Rico did not prosper for the reason that the plant takes a long time in coming to maturity, and during that period is exceedingly sensible to the effects of strong winds, which, in this island, prevail from July to October. The first plantations being destroyed by hurricanes, few new plantations were made.

Of the other staple products of Puerto Rico, the most valuable, coffee, was first planted in Martinique in 1720 by M. Declieux, who brought the seeds from the Botanical Garden in Paris. The coco-palm was introduced by Diego Lorenzo, a canon in the Cape de Verde Islands, who also brought the first guinea-fowls; and, possibly, the plantain species known in this island under the name of "guinéo" came from the same part of the world. According to Oviedo, it was first planted in Santo Domingo in 1516 by a monk named Berlangas.

Abbad gives the detailed agricultural statistics of the island in 1776, from which it appears that the cultivation of the new articles introduced was general at the time, and that, under the influence of climate and abundant pastures, the animal industry had become one of the principal sources of wealth for the inhabitants.

There were in that year 5,581 farms, and 234 cattle-ranches (hatos).

On the farms or estates there were under cultivation:

Sugar-cane 3,156 cuerdas[70]
Plantains 8,315 "
Coffee-trees 1,196,184
Cotton-plants 103,591

On the cattle-ranches there were:
Head of horned cattle 77,384
Horses 23,195
Mules 1,534
Asses, swine, goats, and sheep 49,050

102

This was a comparatively large capital in stock and produce for a population of 80,000 souls, but the reverend historian severely criticizes the agricultural population of that day, and says of them: " ... They scarcely know what implements are; ... they bring down a tree, principally by means of fire; with a saber, which they call a 'machete,' they clear the jungle and clean the ground; with the point of this machete, or a pointed stick, they dig the holes or furrows in which they set their plants or sow their seeds. Thus they provide for their subsistence, and when a hurricane or other mishap destroys their crops, they supply their wants by fishing or collect edible roots.

"Indolence, rather than want of means, makes them confine their cultivation to the level lands, which they abandon as soon as they perceive that the fertility of the soil decreases, which happens very soon, because they do not plow, nor do they turn over the soil, much less manure it, so that the superficies soon becomes sterile; then they make a clearing on some mountainside. Neither the knowledge of the soil and climate acquired during many years of residence, nor the increased facilities for obtaining the necessary agricultural implements, nor the large number of cattle they possess that could be used for agricultural purposes, nor the Government's dispositions to improve the system of cultivation, have been sufficient to make these islanders abandon the indolence with which they regard the most important of all arts, and the first obligation imposed by God on man— namely, the cultivation of the soil. They leave this to the slaves, who are few and ill-fed, and know no more of agriculture than their masters do; ... their great laziness, together with a silly, baseless vanity, makes them look upon all manual labor as degrading, proper only for slaves, and so they prefer poverty to doing honest work. To this must be added their ambition to make rapid fortunes, as some of them do, by contraband trading, which makes good sailors of them but bad agriculturists.

"These are the reasons why they prefer the cultivation of produce that requires little labor. Most proprietors have a small portion of their land planted with cane, but few have made it their principal crop, because of the expense of erecting a mill and the greater number of slaves and implements required; yet this industry alone, if properly fostered, would soon remove all obstacles to their progress.

"It is useless, therefore, to look for gardens and orchards in a country where the plow is yet unknown, and which has not even made the first step in agricultural development."

* * * * *

Under the royal decree of 1815 commerce, both foreign and inland, rapidly developed.

From the official returns made to the Government in 1828 to 1830, Colonel Flinter drew up the following statement of the agricultural wealth of the island in the latter year (1830):

Wooden sugar-cane mills 1,277
Iron sugar-cane mills 800
Coffee estates with machinery 148
Stills for distilling rum 340

103

Brick ovens 80

Lime kilns 45

Land under Cultivation

Cane 14,803 acres.

Plantains 30,706 "

Rice 14,850 "

Maize 16,194 "

Tobacco 2,599 "

Manioc 1,150 "

Sweet potatoes 1,224 "

Yams 6,696 "

Pulse 1,100 "

Horticulture 31 "

  Coffee-plants 16,750 acres 16,992,857

Cotton-trees 3,079 " 3,079,310

Coco-palms 2,402 " 60,050

Orange-trees 3,430 " 85,760

Aguacate-trees 2,230 " 55,760

Pepper or chilli or aji trees 500

  The live stock of the island in the same year consisted of:

Cows 42,500 head.

Bulls 6,720 "

Oxen 20,910 "

Horses 25,760 "

Mares 27,210 "

Asses 315 "

Mules 1,112 "

Sheep 7,560 "

Goats 5,969 "

Swine 25,087 "

Turkeys 8,671 "

Other fowls 838,454 "

  This agricultural wealth of the island, houses, lands, and slaves *not* included, was valued at $37,993,600, and its annual produce at $6,883,371, half of which was exported. These statistics may be considered as only *approximately correct,* as the returns made by the proprietors to the Government, in order to escape taxation, were less than the real numbers existing.

  The natural wealth of Puerto Rico may be divided into agricultural, pastoral, and sylvan. According to the Spanish Government measurements the island's area is 2,584,000 English acres. Of these, there were

Under cultivation in 1830, as above

detailed 117,244 acres.

In pastures 634,506 "

In forests 728,703 "

Total *tax-paying lands* 1,480,453 "

The pasture lands on the north and east coasts are equal to the best lands of the kind in the West Indies for the breeding and fattening of cattle. On the south coast excessive droughts often parch the grass, in which case the cattle are fed on cane-tops at harvest time. There are excellent and nutritive native grasses of different species to be found in every valley. The cattle bred in the island are generally tame.

From 1865 to 1872 was the era of greatest prosperity ever experienced in Puerto Rico under Spanish rule. The land was not yet exhausted, harvests were abundant, labor cheap, the quality of the sugar produced was excellent, prices were high, contributions and taxes were moderate. There were no export duties, and although, during this period, the growing manufacture of beet-root sugar was lowering the price of "mascabado" all over the world, no effect was felt in Puerto Rico, because it was the nearest market to the United States, where the civil war had put an end to the annual product by the Southern States of half a million bocoyes,[71] or about 675,000,000 gallons; and the abolition of all import duties on sugar in England also favored the maintenance of high prices for a number of years.

However, the production of beet-root sugar and the increase of cane cultivation in the East[72] caused the fall in prices which, in combination with the numberless oppressive restrictions imposed by the Spanish Government, brought Puerto Rico to the verge of ruin.

"The misfortunes that afflict us," says Mr. James McCormick to the Provincial Deputation in his official report on the condition of the sugar industry in this island in 1880, "come under different forms from different directions, and *every inhabitant knows what causes have contributed to reduce this island, once prosperous and happy, to its actual condition of prostration and anguish.*"

That condition he paints in the following words: "Mechanical arts and industries languish because there is no demand or profitable market for its products; commerce is paralyzed by the obstacles placed in its way; the country never has had sufficient capital and what there is hides itself or is withdrawn from circulation; foreign capital has been frightened away; Puerto Rican landowners are looked upon with special disfavor and credit is denied them, unfortunately with good reason, seeing the lamentable condition of our agriculture. The production of sugar scarcely amounts to half of what it was in former years. From the year 1873 a great proportion of the existing sugar estates have fallen to ruin; in 8 districts their number has been reduced from 104 to 38, and of these the majority are in an agonizing condition. In other parts of the island many estates, in which large capitals in machinery, drainage, etc., have been invested, have been abandoned and the land is returning to its primitive condition of jungle and swamp. Ten years ago the island exported 100,000 tons of sugar annually, the product of 553 mills; during the last three years (1878-1880) the average export has been 60,000 tons, the product of 325 mills that have been able to continue working. Everywhere in this province the evidences of the ruin which has overtaken the planters meet the eye, and nothing is heard but the lamentations of proprietors reduced to misery and desperation."

This state of things continued notwithstanding the representations made before the "high spheres of Government" by the leading men in commerce and agriculture, by the press of all political colors, and by Congress. The Minister of Ultramar in Madrid recognized the gravity of the situation, and it is said that the lamentations of the people of Puerto Rico found an echo even at the foot of the throne.

And there they died. Nothing was done to remedy the growing evil, and the writer of the pamphlet, not daring openly to accuse the Government as the only cause of the island's desperate situation, counsels patience, and timidly expresses the hope that the exorbitant taxes and contributions will be lowered; that economy in the Government expenditures will be practised; that monopolies will be abolished, and odious, oppressive practises of all kinds be discontinued.

Such was the condition of Puerto Rico in 1880. The Government's oppressive practises, and they only, were the causes of the ruin of this and all the other rich and beautiful colonies that destiny laid at the feet of Ferdinand and Isabel four centuries ago.

The following statement of the proportion of sugar to each acre of land under cane cultivation in the Antilles, compared with Puerto Rico, may be of interest.

The computation of the average sugar produce per acre, according to the best and most correct information from intelligent planters, who had no motives for deception, was, in 1830:[73]

For Jamaica 10 centals per acre.
Dominica 10 " "
Granada 15 " "
St. Vincent 25 " "
Tobago 20 " "
Antigua 7-12 " "
Saint Kitts 20 " "
Puerto Rico 30 " "

FOOTNOTES:

[Footnote 69: Leyes de Indias, Ley IV, Libro IV, Titulo XVIII.]

[Footnote 70: The actual cuerda is a square of 75 varas each side, about one-tenth less than an acre. Abbad understood by a cuerda a rectangle of 75 varas front by 1,500 varas depth, that is, 20 cuerdas superficies of those actually in use. —*Acosta*.]

[Footnote 71: The bocoy in Puerto Rico, equal from 12 to 20 centals of sugar, according the quality.]

[Footnote 72: British India produced about that time over 1,500,000 tons of cane-sugar per annum.]

[Footnote 73: Colonel Flinter, An Account of the Island of Puerto Rico. London, 1834]

106

CHAPTER XXXIV
COMMERCE AND FINANCES

Until the year 1813 the captains-general of Puerto Rico had the superintendence of the revenues. The capital was the only authorized port open to commerce. No regular books were kept by the authorities. A day-book of duties paid and expended was all that was considered necessary. Merchandise was smuggled in at every part of the coast,[74] the treasury chest was empty, and the Government officers and troops were reduced to a very small portion of their pay.

The total revenues of the island, including the old-established taxes and contributions, produced 70,000 pesos, and half of that sum was never recovered on account of the abuses and dishonesty that had been introduced in the system of collection.

An intendancy was deemed necessary, and the Home Government appointed Alexander Ramirez to the post in February, 1813. He promptly introduced important reforms in the administration, and caused regular accounts to be kept. He made ample and liberal concessions to commerce, opened five additional ports with custom-houses, freed agriculture from the trammels that had impeded its development, and placed labor, instruments, seeds, and modern machinery within its reach. He printed and distributed short essays or manuals on the cultivation of different products and the systems adopted by other nations, promoted the immigration of Canary Islanders, founded the Royal Economic Society of Friends of the Country, and edited the Diario Económico de Puerto Rico, the first number of which appeared February 28, 1814.

The first year after the establishment of these improvements, notwithstanding the abolition of some of the most onerous taxes, the revenues of the capital rose to $161,000, and the new custom-houses produced $242,842.

Having placed this island's financial administration on a sound basis, Ramirez was called upon by the Government to perform the same valuable services for Cuba. Unfortunately, his successors here soon destroyed the good effects of his measures by continual variations in the system, and in the commercial tariffs. They attempted to prevent smuggling by increasing the duties, the very means of encouraging contraband trade, and the old mismanagement and malversations in the custom-houses revived. One intendant, often from a mere spirit of innovation, applied to the court for a decree canceling the regulations of his predecessor, so that, from the concurring effects of contraband and mismanagement, commerce suffered, and the country became once more impoverished.

The revenues fell so low and the malversation of public money reached such a height that the captain-general found it necessary in 1825 to charge the military commanders of the respective districts with the prevention of smuggling. He placed supervisors of known intelligence and probity in each custom-house to watch and prevent fraud and peculation. These measures almost doubled the amount of revenue in the following year (1826).

As late as 1810 the imports in Puerto Rico exceeded three times the sum of the produce exported. The difference was made up by the "situados," or remittances in cash from Mexico, which began early in the seventeenth century, when the repeated attacks on the island by French and English privateers forced the Spanish Government to choose between losing the island or fortifying it. The king chose the latter, and made an assignment on the royal treasury of Mexico of nearly half a million pesos per annum. With these subsidies all the fortifications were constructed and the garrison and civil and military employees were paid, till the insurrection in Mexico put a stop to the fall of this pecuniary manna.

It was fortunate for Puerto Rico that it ceased. The people of the island had become so accustomed to look to this supply of money for the purchase of their necessities that they entirely neglected the development of the rich resources in their fertile soil. When a remittance arrived in due time, all was joy and animation; when it was delayed, as was often the case, all was gloom and silence, and recourse was had to "papeletas," a temporary paper currency or promises to pay.

With the cessation of the "situados" the scanty resources of the treasury soon gave out. The funds of the churches were first requisitioned; then the judicial deposits, the property of people who had died in the Peninsula, and other unclaimed funds were attached; next, donations and private loans were solicited, and when all these expedients were exhausted, the final resort of bankrupt communities, paper money, was adopted (1812).

Then Puerto Rico's poverty became extreme. In 1814 there was at least half a million paper money in circulation with a depreciation of 400 per cent. To avoid absolute ruin, the intendant had recourse to the introduction of what were called "macuquinos," or pieces of rudely cut, uncoined silver of inferior alloy, representing approximately the value of the coin that each piece of metal stood for. With these he redeemed in 1816 all the paper money that had been put in circulation; but the emergency money gave rise to agioist speculation and remained the currency long after it had served its purpose. It was not replaced by Spanish national coin till 1857.

The royal decree of 1815, and the improvements in the financial situation, as a result of the new administrative system established by Ramirez, gave a strong impulse to foreign commerce. Though commerce with the mother country remained in a languishing condition, because the so-called "decree of graces" had fixed the import duty on Spanish merchandise at 6 per cent *ad valorem*, while the valuations which the custom-house officials made exceeded the market prices to such an extent that many articles really paid 8 per cent and some 10, 12, and even 15 per cent.

An estimate of the commerce of this island about the year 1830 divides the total imports and exports which, in that year, amounted to $5,620,786 among the following nations:

Per cent. Per cent.
West Indian Islands imports 53-12 Exports 26
United States imports 27-14 " 49
Spanish imports 12-18 " 7

108

English imports 2-34 " 6-12
French imports 2-58 " 6-58
Other nations' imports 1-34 " 8-34

The American trade at that time formed nearly one-third of the whole of the value of the imports and nearly half of all the exports.

An American consul resided at the capital and all the principal ports had deputy consuls. The articles of importation from the United States were principally timber, staves for sugar-casks, flour and other provisions, and furniture.[75]

* * * * *

The financial history of Puerto Rico commences about the middle of the eighteenth century. In 1758 the revenues amounted to 6,858 pesos. In 1765, to 10,814, and in 1778 to 47,500. Their increase up to 1,605,523 in 1864 was due to the natural development of the island's resources, which accompanied the increase of population; yet financial distress was chronic all the time, and not a year passed without the application of the supposed panacea of royal decrees and ordinances, without the expected improvement.

From 1850 to 1864, for the first time in the island's history, there happened to be a surplus revenue. The authorities wasted it in an attempt to reannex Santo Domingo and in contributions toward the expenses of the war in Morocco. The balance was used by the Spanish Minister of Ultramar, the Government being of opinion that surpluses in colonial treasuries were a source of danger. To avoid a plethora of money contributions were asked for in the name of patriotism, which nobody dared refuse, and which were, therefore, always liberally responded to. Of this class was a contribution of half a million pesos toward the expenses of the war with the Carlists to secure the succession of Isabel II, and Sunday collections for the benefit of the Spanish soldiers in Cuba, for the sufferers by the inundations in Murcia, the earthquakes in Andalusia, etc. From 1870 to 1876 a series of laws and ordinances relating to finances were promulgated. February 22d, a royal decree admitted Mexican silver coin as currency. December 3, 1880, another royal decree reformed the financial administration of the island. This was followed in 1881 by instructions for the collection of personal contributions. In 1882 the Intendant Alcázar published the regulations for the imposition, collection, and administration of the land tax; from 1882 to 1892 another series of laws, ordinances, and decrees appeared for the collection and administration of different taxes and contributions, and October 28, 1895, another royal decree withdrew the Mexican coin from circulation. In the same year (March 15th) the reform laws were promulgated, which were followed in the next year by the municipal law.[76]

In the meantime commerce languished. The excessively high export duties on island produce imposed by Governor Sanz in 1868 to 1870 brought 600,000 pesos per annum into the treasury, but ruined agriculture, and this lasted till the end of Spanish rule.

The directory of the Official Chamber of Commerce, Industry, and Navigation of San Juan, at the general meeting of members in 1895, reported that it had occupied itself during that year, through the medium of the island's representative

109

in Cortes, with the promised tariff reform, but without result. Nor had its endeavors to obtain the exchange of the Mexican coin still in circulation for Peninsular money been successful on account of the opposition of those interested in the maintenance of the system. The abolition of the so-called "conciertos" of matches and petroleum had also occupied them, and in this case successfully; but the directors complained of the apathy and the indifference of the public in general for the objects which the Chamber of Commerce was organized to advocate and promote, and they state that within the last year the number of associates had diminished.

The Directors' report of January, 1897, was even more gloomy. They complain of the want of interest in their proceedings on the part of many of the leading commercial houses, of the lamentable condition of commerce, of the inattention of their "mother," Spain, to the plausible pretentions of this her daughter, animated though she was by the most fervent patriotism.

FOOTNOTES:

[Footnote 74: Rafael Conty, subdelegate of the treasury of Aguadilla, sailed round the island in a sloop in 1790 and confiscated eleven vessels engaged in smuggling.]

[Footnote 75: For commercial statistics of Puerto Rico from 1813 to 1864, see Señor Acosta's interesting notes to Chapter XXVIII of Abbad's history.]

[Footnote 76: *Vide* Reseña del Estado Social, Económico é Industrial de la Isla de Puerto Rico por el Dr. Cayetano Coll y Toste, 1899.]

CHAPTER XXXV
EDUCATION IN PUERTO RICO

In Chapter XXIII of this history we gave an extract from his Excellency Alexander O'Reilly's report to King Charles IV, wherein, referring to the intellectual status of the inhabitants of Puerto Rico in 1765, he informs his Majesty that there were only two schools in the whole island and that, outside of the capital and San German, few knew how to read.

In the mother country, at that period, even primary instruction was very deficient. It remained so for a long time. As late as 1838 reading, writing, and arithmetic only were taught in the best public schools of Spain. The other branches of knowledge, such as geography, history, physics, chemistry, natural history, could be studied in a few ecclesiastical educational establishments.[77] The illiteracy of the inhabitants of this, the least important of Spain's conquered provinces, was therefore but natural, seeing that the conquerors who had settled in it belonged to the most ignorant classes of an illiterate country in an illiterate age. Something was done in Puerto Rico by the Dominican and Franciscan friars in the way of preparatory training for ecclesiastical callings. They taught Latin and philosophy to a limited number of youths; the bishop himself gave regular instruction in Latin.

A few youths, whose parents could afford it, were sent to the universities of Carácas and Santo Domingo, where some of them distinguished themselves by their aptitude for study. One of these, afterward known as Father Bonilla,

110

obtained the highest academic honors in Santo Domingo.

From 1820 to 1823, under the auspices of a constitutional government, intellectual life in Puerto Rico really began. A Mr. Louis Santiago called public attention to the necessity of attending to primary education. "The greatest evil," he said, "that which demands the speediest remedy, is the general ignorance of the art of reading and writing. It is painful to see the signatures of the alcaldes to public documents." He wrote a pamphlet of instructions in the art of teaching in primary schools, which was printed and distributed through the interior of the island. The governor, Gonzalo Arostegui, addressed an official note to the Provincial Deputation charging that body to propose to him "without rest or interruption, and as soon as possible," the means to establish primary schools in the capital and in the towns of the interior; to the municipalities he sent a circular, dated September 28, 1821, recommending them to facilitate the coming to the capital of the teachers in their respective districts who wished to attend, for a period of two months, a class in the Lancasterian method of primary teaching, to be held in the Normal School by Ramon Carpegna, the political secretary. A certain amount of instruction, talent, and disposition for magisterial work was required of the pupils, and those who already had positions as teachers could assist at the two months' course without detriment to their salaries.

The fall of the constitutional government in Spain, brought about by French intervention and the reaction that followed, extinguished the light that had just begun to shine, and this unfortunate island was again plunged into the intellectual darkness of the middle ages. Persecution became fiercer than ever, and the citizens most distinguished for their learning and liberal ideas had to seek safety in emigration.

For the next twenty years the education of the youth of Puerto Rico was entirely in the hands of the clergy. With the legacies left to the Church by Bishop Arizmendi and other pious defuncts, Bishop Pedro Gutierrez de Cos founded the Conciliar Seminary in 1831, and appointed as Rector Friar Angel de la Concepción Vazquez, a Puerto Rican by birth, educated in the Franciscan Convent of Carácas.

In the same year there came to Puerto Rico, as prebendary of the cathedral, an ex-professor of experimental physics in the University of Galicia, whose name was Rufo Fernandez. He founded a cabinet of physics and a chemical laboratory, and invited the youth of the capital to attend the lectures on these two sciences which he gave gratis.

Fray Angel, as he was familiarly called, the rector of the seminary, at Dr. Rufo's suggestion, asked permission of the superior ecclesiastical authorities to transfer the latter's cabinet and laboratory to the seminary for the purpose of adding the courses of physics and chemistry to the curriculum, but failed to obtain it, the reasons given for the adverse decision being, "that the science of chemistry was unnecessary for the students, who, in accordance with the dispositions of the Council of Trent, were to dedicate themselves to ecclesiastical sciences only." The rector, while expressing his regret at the decision, adds: "I can not help telling you what I have always felt—namely, that there is some malediction resting on the

111

education of youth in this island, which evokes formidable obstacles from every side, though there are not wanting generous spirits ready to make sacrifices in its favor." [78]

Some of these generous spirits had organized, as early as 1813, under the auspices of Intendant Ramirez, the Economic Society of Friends of the Country. Puerto Rico owes almost all its intellectual progress to this society. Its aim was the island's moral and material advancement, and, in spite of obstacles, it has nobly labored with that object in view to the end of Spanish domination. From its very inception it established a primary school for 12 poor girls, and classes in mathematics, geography, French, English, and drawing, to which a class of practical or applied mechanics was added later. In 1844 the society asked and obtained permission from the governor, the Count of Mirasol, to solicit subscriptions for the establishment and endowment of a central college. The people responded with enthusiasm, and in less than a month 30,000 pesos were collected.

The college was opened. In 1846 four youths, under the guidance of Dr. Rufo, were sent to Spain to complete their studies to enable them to worthily fill professorships in the central school. Two of them died shortly after their arrival in Madrid. When the other two returned to Puerto Rico in 1849 they found the college closed and the subscriptions for its maintenance returned to the donors by order of Juan de la Pezuela, Count Mirasol's successor in the governorship.

If the unfavorable opinion of the character of the Puerto Ricans to which this personage gave expression in one of his official communications was the motive for his proceeding in this case, it would seem that he changed it toward the end of his administration, for he founded a Royal Academy of Belles-Lettres, and a library which was provided with books by occasional gifts from the public. He introduced some useful reforms in the system of primary instruction, and inaugurated the first prize competitions for poetical compositions by native authors.

From the returns of the census of 1860 it appears that at that time only 17-12 per cent of the male population of the island knew how to read, and only 12-12 per cent of the female population. Four years later, at the end of 1864 there were, according to official data, 98,817 families in Puerto Rico whose intellectual wants were supplied by 74 public schools for boys and 48 for girls, besides 16 and 9 private schools for boys and girls respectively.

In 1854 General Norzagery, then governor, assisted by Andres Viña, the secretary of the Royal Board of Commerce and Industry, had founded a school of Commerce, Agriculture, and Navigation. After sixteen years of existence, this establishment was unfavorably reported upon by Governor Sanz, who wished to suppress it on account of the liberal ideas and autonomist tendencies of its two principal professors, José Julian Acosta (Abbad's commentator) and Ramon B. Castro. In the preamble to a secret report sent by this governor to Madrid he says: "This supreme civil government has always secured professors who, in addition to the required ability for their position, possess the moral and political character and qualities to form citizens, lovers of their country, i.e., lovers of Puerto Rico as a

112

Spanish province, *not of Puerto Rico as an independent state annexed to North America.*"

Female education had all along received even less attention than the education of boys. Alexander Infiesta, in an article on the subject published in the Revista in February, 1888, states, that according to the latest census there were 399,674 females in the island, of whom 293,247 could neither read nor write, 158,528 of them being white women and girls. The number of schools for boys was 408, with an attendance of 18,194, and that for girls 127, with 7,183 pupils.

From the memorial published by the Director of the Provincial Institute for Secondary Education, regarding the courses of study in that establishment during the year 1888-'89, we learn that the number of primary schools in the island had increased to 600, but, according to Mr. Coll y Toste's Reseña, published in 1899, there were, among a total population of 894,302 souls, only 497 primary schools in the island at the time of the American occupation. The total attendance was 22,265 pupils, 15,108 boys and 7,157 girls.

FOOTNOTES:

[Footnote 77: See Franco del Valle Atilés, Causas del atras Intelectual del campesino Puertoriqueño. Revista Puertoriqueña, Año II, tomo II, p. 7.]

[Footnote 78: Letter to Dr. Rufo Fernandez from Fray Angel de la Concepcion Vazquez. See Acosta's notes to Abbad's history, pp. 412, 413, foot note.]

CHAPTER XXXVI
LIBRARIES AND THE PRESS

Books for the people were considered by the Spanish colonial authorities to be of the nature of inflammable or explosive substances, which it was not safe to introduce freely.

From their point of view, they were right. The Droits de l'homme of Jean Jacques Rousseau, for example, translated into every European language, had added more volunteers of all nationalities to the ranks of the Spanish-American patriots than was generally supposed—and so, books and printing material were subjected to the payment of high import duties, and a series of annoying formalities, among which the passing of the political and ecclesiastical censors was the most formidable.

The result among the poorer classes of natives was blank illiteracy. A pall of profound ignorance hung over the island, and although, with the revival of letters in the seventeenth century the light of intellect dawned over western Europe, not a ray of it was permitted to reach the Spanish colonies.

The ruling class, every individual of whom came from the Peninsula, kept what books each individual possessed to themselves. To the people all learning, except such as it was considered safe to impart, was forbidden fruit.

Under these conditions it is not strange that the idea of founding public libraries did not germinate in the minds of the more intelligent among the Puerto Ricans till the middle of the nineteenth century; whereas, the other colonies that had shaken off their allegiance to the mother country, had long since entered upon the road of intellectual progress with resolute step.

Collegiate libraries, however, had existed in the capital of the island as early as the sixteenth century. The first of which we have any tradition was founded by the Dominican friars in their convent. It contained works on art, literature, and theology.

The next library was formed in the episcopal palace, or "casa parochial," by Bishop Don Bernardo de Valbuena, poet and author of a pastoral novel entitled the Golden Age, and other works of literary merit. This library, together with that of the Dominicans, and the respective episcopal and conventual archives were burned by the Hollanders during the siege of San Juan in 1625.

The Franciscan friars also had a library in their convent (1660). The books disappeared at the time of the community's dissolution in 1835.

Bishop Pedro Gutierres de Cos, who founded the San Juan Conciliar Seminary in 1832, established a library in connection with it, the remains of which are still extant in the old seminary building, but much neglected and worm-eaten.

A library of a semipublic character was founded by royal order dated June 19, 1831, shortly after the installation of the Audiencia in San Juan. It was a large and valuable collection of books on juridical subjects, which remained under the care of a salaried librarian till 1899, when it was amalgamated with the library of the College of Lawyers.

This last is a rich collection of works on jurisprudence, and the exclusive property of the college, but accessible to professional men. The library is in the former Audiencia building, now occupied by the insular courts.

The period from 1830 to 1850 appears to have been one of greatest intellectual activity in Puerto Rico. Toward its close Juan de la Pezuela, the governor, founded the Royal Academy of Belles-Lettres, an institution of literary and pedagogical character, with the functions of a normal school. It was endowed with a modest library, but it only lived till the year 1860, when, in consequence of disagreement between the founder and the professors, the school was closed and the library passed into the possession of the Economic Society of Friends of the Country.

This, and the library of the Royal Academy, which the society had also acquired, formed a small but excellent nucleus, and with, the produce of the public subscription of 1884 it was enabled to stock its library with many of the best standard works of the time in Spanish and French, and open to the Puerto Ricans of all classes the doors of the first long-wished-for public library.

Since then it has contributed in no small degree to the enlightenment of the better part of the laboring classes in the capital, till it was closed at the commencement of the war.

During the transition period the books were transferred from one locality to another, and in the process the best works disappeared, until the island's first civil governor, Charles H. Allen, at the suggestion of Commissioner of Education Martin G. Brumbaugh, rescued the remainder and made it the nucleus of the first *American* free library.

The second Puerto Rican public library was opened by Don Ramon Santaella, October 15, 1880, in the basement of the Town Hall. It began with 400 volumes, and possesses to-day 6,361 literary and didactic books in different languages.

114

The Puerto Rican Atheneum Library was established in 1876. Its collection of books, consisting principally of Spanish and French literature, is an important one, both in numbers and quality. It has been enriched by accessions of books from the library of the extinct Society of Friends of the Country. It is open to members of the Atheneum only, or to visitors introduced by them.

The Casino Español possesses a small but select library with a comfortable reading-room. Its collection of books and periodicals is said to be the richest and most varied in the island. It was founded in 1871.

The religious association known under the name of Conferences of St. Vincent de Paul had a small circulating library of religious works duly approved by the censors. The congregation was broken up in 1887 and the library disappeared.

The Provincial Institute of Secondary Education, which was located in the building now occupied by the free library and legislature, possessed a small pedagogical library which shared the same fate as that of the Society of Friends of the Country.

The Spanish Public Works Department possessed another valuable collection of books, mostly on technical and scientific subjects. A number of books on other than technical subjects, probably from the extinct libraries just referred to, have been added to the original collection, and the whole, to the number of 1,544 volumes in excellent condition, exist under the care of the chief of the Public Works Department.

Besides the above specified libraries of a public and collegiate character, there are some private collections of books in the principal towns of the island. Chief among these is the collection of Don Fernando Juncos, of San Juan, which contains 15,000 volumes of classic and preceptive literature and social and economic science, 1,200 volumes of which bear the author's autographs.

The desire for intellectual improvement began to manifest itself in the interior of the island a few years after the establishment of the first public library in the capital. The municipality of Ponce founded a library in 1894. It contains 809 bound volumes and 669 pamphlets in English, German, French, and Spanish, many of them duplicates. The general condition of the books is bad, and the location of the library altogether unsuitable. There was a municipal appropriation of 350 pesos per annum for library purposes, but since 1898 it has not been available.

Mayaguez founded its public library in 1872. It possesses over 5,000 volumes, with a small archeological and natural history museum attached to it.

Some of the smaller towns also felt the need of intellectual expansion, and tried to supply it by the establishment of reading-rooms. Arecibo, Véga-Baja, Toa-Alta, Yauco, Cabo-Rojo, Aguadilla, Humacáo, and others made efforts in this direction either through their municipalities or private initiative. A few only succeeded, but they did not outlive the critical times that commenced with the war, aggravated by the hurricane of August, 1898.

* * * * *

Since the American occupation of the island, four public libraries have been established. Two of them are exclusively Spanish, the Circulating Scholastic

Library, inaugurated in San Juan on February 22, 1901, by Don Pedro Carlos Timothe, and the Circulating Scholastic Library of Yauco, established a month later under the auspices of S. Egózene of that town. The two others are, one, largely English, the Pedagogical Library, established under the auspices of the Commissioner of Education, and the San Juan Free Library, to which Mr. Andrew Carnegie has given $100,000, and which is polyglot, and was formally opened to the public April 20, 1901. There is also a growing number of libraries in the public schools. From the above data it appears that, owing to the peculiar conditions that obtained in this island, the people of Puerto Rico were very slow in joining the movement of intellectual expansion which began in Spanish America in the eighteenth century. They did so at last, unaided and with their own limited resources, even before the obstacles placed in their way by the Government were removed. If they have not achieved more, it is because within the last few decades the island has been unfortunate in more than one respect. Now that a new era has dawned, it may reasonably be expected that the increased opportunities for intellectual development afforded them will be duly appreciated and taken advantage of by the people, and if we may judge from the eagerness with which the youth of the capital reads the books of the San Juan Free Library, it seems clear that the seed so recently sown has fallen in fruitful soil.

* * * * *

The history of the Press in Puerto Rico is short. The first printing machine was introduced by the Government in 1807 for the purpose of publishing the Official Gazette. No serious attempt at publication of any periodical for the people was made till the commencement of the second constitutional period (1820-'23), when, for the first time in the island's history, public affairs could be discussed without the risk of imprisonment or banishment. The right of association was also recognized. The Society of Liberal Lovers of the Country and the Society of Lovers of Science were formed about this time. The Investigator and the Constitutional Gazette were published and gave food for nightly discussions on political and social questions in the coffee-house on the Marina.

The period of freedom of spoken and written thought was short, but an impulse had been given which could not be arrested. In 1865 there were eight periodicals published in the island. On September 29th of that year a law regulating the publication of newspapers indirectly suppressed half of them. It contained twenty articles, each more stringent than the other. To obtain a license to publish or to continue publishing a paper, a deposit of 2,000 crowns had to be made to cover the fines that were almost sure to be imposed. The publications were subject to the strictest censorship. They could not appear till the proofs of each article had been signed by the censor, and the whole process of printing and publishing was fenced in by such minute and annoying regulations, the smallest infraction of which was punished by such heavy fines that it was a marvel how any paper could be published under such conditions. These conditions were relaxed a decade or two later, and a number of publications sprang into existence at once. When the United States Government took possession of the island, there were 9 periodicals published in San Juan, 5 in Ponce, 3 in Mayaguez, 1 in

116

Humacáo, and a few others in different towns of the interior.

CHAPTER XXXVII
THE REGULAR AND SECULAR CLERGY

In Catholic countries the monastic orders constitute the regular clergy. The secular clergy is not bound by monastic rules. Both classes exercise their functions independently, the former under the authority of their respective superiors or generals, the latter under the bishops.

When, after the return of Columbus from his first voyage, the existence of a new world was demonstrated and preparations for occupying it were made, the Pope, to assure the Christianization of the inhabitants, gave to the monks of all orders who wished to go the privilege, pertaining till then to the secular clergy exclusively, of administering parishes and collecting tithes without subjection to the authority of the bishops.

The Dominicans and the Franciscans availed themselves of this privilege at once. There was rivalry for power and influence between these two orders from the time of their first installation, and they carried their quarrels with them to America, where their differences of opinion regarding the enslaving and treatment of the Indians embittered them still more. The Dominicans secured a footing in Santo Domingo and in Puerto Rico almost to the exclusion of their rivals, notwithstanding the king's recommendation to Ceron in 1511 to build a monastery for Franciscans, whose doctrines he considered "salutary."

Puerto Rico was scantily provided with priests till the year 1518, when the treasurer, Haro, wrote to Cardinal Cisneros: "There are no priests in the granges as has been commanded; only one in Capárra, and one in San German. The island is badly served. Send us a goodly number of priests or permission to pay them out of the produce of the tithes."

The "goodly number of priests" was duly provided. Immediately after the transfer of the capital to its present site in 1521, the Dominicans began the construction of a convent, which was nearly completed in 1529, when there were 25 friars in it. They had acquired great influence over Bishop Manso, and obtained many privileges and immunities from him. Bishop Bastidas, Manso's successor, was less favorably disposed toward them, and demanded payment of tithes of the produce of their agricultural establishments. He reported to the king in 1548: "There is a Dominican monastery here large enough for a city of 2,000 inhabitants,[79] and there are many friars in it. They possess farms, cattle, negroes, Indians, and are building horse-power sugar-mills; meanwhile, I know that they are asking your Majesty for alms to finish their church … It were better to oblige them to sell their estates and live in poverty as prescribed by the rules of their order."

The Franciscans came to Puerto Rico in 1534, but founded no convent till 1585, when one of their order, Nicolas Ramos, was appointed to the see of San Juan. Then they established themselves in "la Aguáda," and named the settlement San Francisco de Asis. Two years later it was destroyed by the Caribs, and five of the brothers martyrized. No attempt at reconstruction of the convent was made. The order abandoned the island and did not return till 1642, when they obtained the Pope's license to establish themselves in the capital. Like the Dominicans, they soon acquired considerable wealth.

The privilege of administering parishes and collecting tithes, which was the principal source of monastic revenues, was canceled by royal schedule June 13, 1757. The monks continued in the full enjoyment of their property till 1835, when all the property of the regular clergy throughout the Peninsula and the colonies was expropriated by the Government. In this island the convents were appropriated only after long and tedious judicial proceedings, in which the Government demonstrated that the transfer was necessary for the public good. Then the convents were used—that of the Dominicans as Audiencia hall, that of the Franciscans as artillery barracks. The intendancy took charge of the administration of the estate of the two communities, the mortmain was canceled, and the transfer duly legalized. A promised indemnity to the two brotherhoods was never paid, but in 1897 a sum of 5,000 pesos annually was added to the insular budget, to be paid to the clergy as compensation for the expropriated estate of the Dominicans in San German. Succeeding political events prevented the payment of this also. The last representatives in this island of the two dispossessed orders died in San Juan about the year 1865.

Bishop Monserrate made an effort to reestablish the order of Franciscans in 1875-'76. Only three brothers came to the island and they, not liking the aspect of affairs, went to South America.

* * * * *

The first head of the secular clergy in Puerto Rico was nominated in 1511. The Catholic princes besought Pope Julius II to make it a bishopric, and recommended as its first prelate Alonzo Manso, canon of Salamanca, doctor in theology, a man held in high esteem at court. His Holiness granted the request, and designated the whole of the island as the diocese, with the principal settlement in it as the see.

The subsequent conquests on the mainland kept adding vast territories to this diocese till, toward the end of the eighteenth century, it included the whole region extending from the upper Orinoco to the Amazon, and from Guiana to the plains of Bogotá. Manso's successors repeatedly represented to the king the absolute impossibility of attending to the spiritual wants of "the lambs that were continually added to the flock." They requested that the see might be transferred to the mainland or that the diocese might be divided in two or more. This was done in 1791, when the diocese of Guiana was created, and Puerto Rico with the island of Vieyques remained as the original one.

The bishop came to San Juan in 1513, and at once began to dispose all that was necessary to give splendor and good government to the first episcopal seat in America. Unfortunately, he arrived at a time when dissension, strife, and immorality were rampant; and when it became known that he was authorized to collect his tithes *in specie*, the opposition of the quarrelsome and insubordinate inhabitants became so violent that the prelate could not exercise his functions, and was forced to return to the Peninsula in 1515. He came back in 1519, invested

118

with the powers of a Provincial Inquisitor, which he exercised till 1539, when he died and was buried in the cathedral, where a monument with an alabaster effigy marked his tomb till 1625, when it was destroyed by the Hollanders.

Rodrigo Bastidas, a native of Santo Domingo, was Manso's successor. He was appointed Bishop of Coro in Venezuela in 1532, but solicited and obtained the see of Puerto Rico in 1542. He was a man of great capacity, virtuous and benevolent. He advised the suppression of the Inquisition, asked the Government for facilities to educate the youth and advance the agricultural interests of his diocese, and commenced the construction of the cathedral. He died in Santo Domingo in 1561, very old and very rich.

Friar Diego de Salamanca, of the order of Augustines, succeeded Bastidas. He continued the construction of the cathedral, but soon returned to the metropolis, leaving the diocese to the care of the Vicar-General, Santa Olaya, till 1585, when the Franciscan friar Nicolas Bamos was appointed to the see. He was the last Bishop of Puerto Rico who united the functions of inquisitor with those of the episcopate, and a zealous burner of heretics. After him the see remained vacant for fourteen years; since then, to the end of the eighteenth century there were 39 consecrated prelates, 9 of whom renounced, or for some other reason did not take possession. The most distinguished among the remaining 30 were: Bernardo Balbuena, poet and author, 1623-'27; Friar Manuel Gimenez Perez, pious, active, and philanthropist, 1770-'84; and Juan Alejo Arismendi, who, according to the Latin inscription on his tomb, was an amiable, religious, upright, zealous, compassionate, learned, decorous, active, leading, benevolent, paternal man. Of the rest little more is known than their names and the dates of their assumption of office and demise.

* * * * *

The year 1842 was, for the secular clergy, one of anxiety for the safety of their long and assiduously accumulated wealth. The members to the number of 17 individuals, including the bishop, drew annual stipends from the insular treasury to the amount of 36,888 pesos, besides which they possessed and still possess a capital of over one and a half millions of pesos, represented by: 1. Vacant chaplaincies. 2. Investments under the head Ecclesiastical Chapter. 3. Idem for account of the Carmelite Sisterhood. 4. Legacies to saints for the purpose of celebrating masses and processions in all the parishes of the island. 5. Pious donations. 6. Fraternities and religious associations for the worship of some special saint. 7. Revenues from an institution known by the name of Third Orders. 8. Capital invested by the founders of the Hospital of the Conception, the income of which is mostly consumed by the nuns of that order. And 9. The ecclesiastical revenues of different kinds in San German.

All this was put in jeopardy by the following decree:

"Doña Isabel II, by the grace of God and the Constitution of the Spanish Monarchy, Queen of Spain, and during her minority Baldomero Espartero, Duke of 'la Victoria' and Morella, Regent of the kingdom, to all who these presents may see and understand, makes known that the Cortes have decreed, and we have sanctioned, as follows:

119

"ARTICLE I. All properties of the secular clergy of whatever class; rights or shares of whatever origin or denomination they may be, or for whatever application or purpose they may have been given, bought, or acquired, are national properties.

"ART. II. The properties, rights, and shares corresponding in any manner to ecclesiastical unions or fraternities, are also national properties.

"ART. III. All estates, rights, and shares of the cathedral, collegiate and parochial clergy and ecclesiastical unions and fraternities referred to in the preceding articles, are hereby declared *for sale.*"

* * * * * The 15 articles that follow specify the properties in detail, the manner of sale, the disposition of the products, administration of rents, etc.

The law was not carried into effect. Espartero, very popular at first, by adopting the principles of the progressist party, forfeited the support of the conservatives —that is, of the clerical party, and the man is not born yet who can successfully introduce into Spain a radical reform of the nature of the one he sanctioned with his signature September 2, 1841. From that moment his overthrow was certain. Narvaez headed the revolution against him, his own officers and men abandoned him, and on July 30, 1843, he wrote his farewell manifesto to the nation on board a British ship of war.

FOOTNOTES:

[Footnote 79: San Juan had only about 100 "vecinos"—that is, white people.]

CHAPTER XXXVIII
THE INQUISITION
1520-1813

Bishop Manso, on his arrival in 1513, found Puerto Rico in a state bordering on anarchy, and after vain attempts to check the prevalent immorality and establish the authority of the Church, he returned to Spain in 1519. The account he gave Cardinal Cisneros of the island's condition suggested to the Grand Inquisitor the obvious remedy of clothing the bishop with the powers of Provincial Inquisitor, which he did.

Diego Torres Vargas, the canon of the San Juan Cathedral, says in his memoirs: "Manso was made inquisitor, and he, being the first, may be said to have been the Inquisitor-General of the Indies; ... the delinquents were brought from all parts to be burned and punished here ... The Inquisition building exists till this day (1647), and until the coming of the Hollanders in 1625 many sambenitos could be seen in the cathedral hung up behind the choir."

These "sambenitos" were sacks of coarse yellow cloth with a large red cross on them, and figures of devils and instruments of torture among the flames of hell. The delinquents, dressed in one of these sacks, bareheaded and barefooted, were made to do penance, or, if condemned to be burned, marched to the place of execution. It is said that in San Juan they were not tied to a stake but enclosed in a hollow plaster cast, against which the faggots were piled,[80] so that they were roasted rather than burned to death. The place for burning the sinners was outside the gate of the fort San Cristobal. Mr. M.F. Juncos believes that the

120

prisons were in the lower part of the Dominican Convent, later the territorial audience and now the supreme court, but Mr. Salvador Brau thinks that they occupied a plot of ground in the angle formed by Cristo Street and the "Caleta" of San Juan.

Of Nicolas Ramos, the last Bishop of Puerto Rico, who united the functions of inquisitor with the duties of the episcopate, Canon Vargas says: " ... He was very severe, burning and punishing, *as was his duty*, some of the people whose cases came before him ..."

It seems that the records of the Inquisition in this island were destroyed and the traditions of its doings suppressed, because nothing is said regarding them by the native commentators on the island's history. Only the names of a few of the leading men who came in contact with the Tribunal have come down to us. Licentiate Sancho Velasquez, who was accused of speaking against the faith and eating meat in Lent, appears to have been Manso's first victim, since he died in a dungeon. A clergyman named Juan Carecras was sent to Spain at the disposition of the general, for the crime of practising surgery. In the same year (1536) we find the treasurer, Blas de Villasante, in an Inquisition dungeon, because, though married in Spain, he cohabited with a native woman—an offense too common at that time not to leave room for suspicion that the treasurer must have made himself obnoxious to the Holy Office in some other way. In 1537, a judge auditor was sent from the Española, but the parties whose accounts were to be audited contrived to have him arrested by the officers of the Inquisition on the day of his arrival. Doctor Juan Blazquez, having attempted to correct some abuses committed by the Admiral's employees in connivance with the Inquisition agents, suffered forty days' imprisonment, and was condemned to hear a mass standing erect all the time, besides paying a fine of 50 pesos.

These are the only cases on record. Only the walls of the Inquisition building, could they speak, could reveal what passed within them from the time of Manso's arrival in 1520 to the end of the sixteenth century, when the West Indian Superior Tribunal was transferred to Cartagena, and a special subordinate judge only was left in San Juan. Bishop Rodrigo de Bastidas, who visited San Juan on a Government commission in 1533, perceiving the abuses that were committed in the inquisitor's name, proposed the abolition of the Holy Office; but the odious institution continued to exist till 1813, when the extraordinary Cortes of Cadiz removed, for a time, this blot on Spanish history. The decree is dated February 22d, and accompanied by a manifesto which is an instructive historical document in itself. It shows that the Cortes dared not attempt the suppression of the dreaded Tribunal without first convincing the people of the disconnection of the measure with the religious question, and justifying it as one necessary for the public weal.

"You can not doubt," they say, "that we endeavor to maintain in this kingdom the Catholic, Apostolic, Roman religion, which you have the happiness to profess; ... the deputies elected by you know, as do the legislators of all times and all nations, that a social edifice not founded on religion, is constructed in vain; ... the true religion which we profess is the greatest blessing which God has bestowed

121

on the Spanish people; we do not recognize as Spaniards those who do not profess it ... It is the surest support of all private and social virtues, of fidelity to the laws and to the monarch, of the love of country and of just liberty, which are graven in every Spanish heart, which have impelled you to battle with the hosts of the usurper, vanquishing and annihilating them, while braving hunger and nakedness, torture, and death."

The Inquisition is next referred to. It is stated that in their constant endeavor to hasten the termination of the evils that afflict the Spanish nation, the people's representatives have first given their attention to the Inquisition; that, with the object of discovering the exact civil and ecclesiastical status of the Holy Office, they have examined all the papal bulls and other documents that could throw light on the subject, and have discovered that only the Inquisitor-General had ecclesiastical powers; that the Provincial Inquisitors were merely his delegates acting under his instructions; that no supreme inquisitorial council had ever been instituted by papal brief, and that the general, being with the enemy (the French troops), no Inquisition really existed. From these investigations the Cortes had acquired a knowledge of the mode of procedure of the tribunals, of their history, and of the opinion of them entertained by the Cortes of the kingdom in early days. " ... We will now speak frankly to you," continues the document, "for it is time that you should know the naked truth, and that the veil be lifted with which false politicians have covered their designs.

"Examining the instructions by which the provincial tribunals were governed, it becomes clear at first sight that the soul of the institution was inviolable secrecy. This covered all the proceedings of the inquisitors, and made them the arbiters of the life and honor of all Spaniards, without responsibility to anybody on earth. They were men, and as such subject to the same errors and passions as the rest of mankind, and it is inconceivable that the nation did not exact responsibility since, in virtue of the temporal power that had been delegated to them, they condemned to seclusion, imprisonment, torture, and death. Thus the inquisitors exercised a power which the Constitution denies to every authority in the land save the sacred person of the king.

"Another notable circumstance made the power of the Inquisitors-General still more unusual; this was that, without consulting the king or the Supreme Pontiff, they dictated laws, changed them, abolished them, or substituted them by others, so that there was within the nation a judge, the Inquisitor-General, whose powers transcended those of the sovereign.

"Here now how the Tribunal proceeded with the offenders. When an accusation was made, the accused were taken to a secret prison without being permitted to communicate with parents, children, relations, or friends, till they were condemned or absolved. Their families were denied the consolation of weeping with them over their misfortunes or of assisting them in their defense. The accused was not only deprived of the assistance of his relations and friends, but in no case was he informed of the name of his accuser nor of the witnesses who declared against him; and in order that he might not discover who they were, they used to truncate the declarations and make them appear as coming from a third

122

party.

"Some one will be bold enough to say that the rectitude and the religious character of the inquisitors prevented the confusion of the innocent with the criminal; but the experiences of many years and the history of the Inquisition give the lie to such assurances. They show us sage and saintly men in the Tribunal's dungeons. Sixtus IV himself, who, at the request of the Catholic kings, had sanctioned the creation of the Tribunal, complained strongly of the innumerable protests that reached him from persecuted people who had been falsely accused of heresy. Neither the virtue nor the position of distinguished men could protect them. The venerable Archbishop of Grenada, formerly the confessor of Queen Isabel, suffered most rigorous persecutions from the inquisitors of Cordóva, and the same befell the Archbishop of Toledo, Friar Louis de Leon, the venerable Avila, Father Siguenza, and many other eminent men.

"In view of these facts, it is no paradox to say that *the ignorance, the decadence of science, of the arts, commerce and agriculture, the depopulation and poverty of Spain, are mainly due to the Inquisition.*

"How the Inquisition could be established among such a noble and generous people as the Spanish, will be a difficult problem for posterity to solve. It will be more difficult still to explain how such a Tribunal could exist for more than three hundred years. Circumstances favored its establishment. It was introduced under the pretext of restraining the Moors and the Jews, who were obnoxious to the Spanish people, and who found protection in their financial relations with the most illustrious families of the kingdom. With such plausible motives the politicians of the time covered a measure which was contrary to the laws of the monarchy. Religion demanded it as a protection, and the people permitted it, though not without strong protest. As soon as the causes that called the Inquisition into existence had ceased, the people's attorneys in Cortes demanded the establishment of the legal mode of procedure. The Cortes of Valladolid of 1518 and 1523 asked from the king that in matters of religion the ordinary judges might be declared competent, and that in the proceedings the canons and common codes might be followed; the Cortes of Saragossa asked the same in 1519, and the kings would have acceded to the will of the people, expressed through their representatives, especially in view of the indirect encouragement to do so which they received from the Holy See, but for the influence of those with whom they were surrounded who had an interest in the maintenance of the odious institution."

The manifesto terminates with an assurance to the Spanish people that, under the new law, heresy would not go unpunished; that, under the new system of judicial proceedings, the innocent would no longer be confounded with the criminal. " ... There will be no more voluntary errors, no more suborned witnesses, offenders will henceforth be judged by upright magistrates in accordance with the sacred canons and the civil code ... Then, genius and talent will display all their energies without fear of being checked in their career by intrigue and calumny; ... science, the arts, agriculture, and commerce will flourish under the guidance of the distinguished men who abound in Spain ... The king,

123

the bishops, all the venerable ecclesiastics will instruct the faithful in the Roman Catholic Apostolic religion without fear of seeing its beauty tarnished by ignorance and superstition, and, who knows, this decree may contribute to the realization, some day, of religious fraternity among all nations!"

From this beautiful dream the Cortes were rudely awakened the very next year when King Ferdinand VII, replaced on his throne by the powers who formed the holy alliance, entered Madrid surrounded by a host of retrograde, revengeful priests. Then the Regency, the Cortes, the Constitution were ignored. The deputies were the first to suffer exile, imprisonment, and death in return for their loyalty and liberalism; the public press was silenced; the convents reopened, municipalities and provincial deputations abolished, the Jesuits restored, the Inquisition reestablished, and priestcraft once more spread its influence over the mental and social life of a naturally generous, brave, and intelligent people.

FOOTNOTES:
[Footnote 80: Neumann, p. 205.]

CHAPTER XXXIX
GROWTH OF CITIES

The proceedings in the formation of a Spanish settlement in the sixteenth century were the same everywhere. For the choice of a site the presence of gold was a condition *sine quâ non*, without gold, no matter how beautiful or fertile the region, no settlement was made.

When a favorable locality was found the first thing done was to construct a fort, because the natives, friendly disposed at first, were not long in becoming the deadly enemies of the handful of strangers who constituted themselves their masters. The next requisite was a church or chapel in which to invoke the divine blessing on the enterprise, or maybe to appease the divine wrath at the iniquities committed. Last, but certainly not least in importance, came the smelting-house, where the King of Spain's share of the gold was separated.

Around these the settlers grouped their houses or huts as they pleased.

The first settlement on this island was made in 1508, on the north coast, at the distance of more than a league from the present port of San Juan, the space between being swampy. Ponce called it Capárra. When the promising result of Ponce's first visit to the island was communicated to King Ferdinand by Ovando, the Governor of la Española, his Highness replied in a letter dated Valladolid, September 15, 1509: "I note the good services rendered by Ponce and that he has not gone to settle the island for want of means. Now that they are being sent from here in abundance, let him go at once with as many men as he can." To Ponce himself the king wrote: "I have seen your letter of August 16th. Be very diligent in the search for gold-mines. Take out as much as possible, smelt it in la Española and remit it instantly. Settle the island as best you can. Write often and let me know what is needed and what passes."

Armed with these instructions, and with his appointment as governor *ad interim*, Ponce returned to San Juan in February, 1510, with his wife and two daughters, settled in Capárra, where, before his departure in 1509, he had built a house of stamped earth (tapia), and where some of the companions of his first expedition had resided ever since. Ponce's house, afterward built of stone, served as a fort. A church or chapel existed already, and we know that there was a smelting-house, because we read that the first gold-smelting took place in Capárra in October, 1510, and that the king's one-fifth came to 2,645 pesos.

With the reinstatement of Ceron and Diaz, complaints about the distance of the settlement from the port, and its unhealthy location, soon reached the king's ears, accompanied by requests for permission to transfer it to an islet near the shore. No action was taken. In November, 1511, the monarch wrote to Ceron: "Ponce says that he founded the town of Capárra in the most favorable locality of the island. I fear that you want to change it. You shall not do so without our special approval. If there is just reason for moving you must first inform me."

Capárra remained for the time the only settlement, and was honored with the name of "City of Puerto Rico." A municipal council was installed, and the king granted the island a coat of arms which differed slightly from that used by the authorities till lately.

The next settlement was made on the south shore, at a place named Guánica, "where there is a bay," says Oviedo, "which is one of the best in the world, but the mosquitoes were so numerous that they alone were sufficient to depopulate it." [81] The Spaniards then moved to Aguáda, on the northwestern shore, and founded a settlement to which they gave the name of their leader Soto Mayor.

This was a young man of aristocratic birth, ex-secretary of King Philip, surnamed "the Handsome." He had come to the Indies with a license authorizing him to traffic in captive Indians, and Ponce, wishing, no doubt, to enlist the young hidalgo's family influence at the court in his favor, made him high constable (*alguacil mayor*) of the southern division (June, 1510).

The new settlement's existence was short. It was destroyed by the Indians in the insurrection of February of the following year, when Christopher Soto Mayor and 80 more of his countrymen, who had imprudently settled in isolated localities in the interior, fell victims of the rage of the natives.

Diego Columbus proposed the reconstruction of the destroyed settlement, with the appellation of San German. The king approved, and near the end of the year 1512, Miguel del Torro, one of Ponce's companions, was delegated to choose a site. He fixed upon the bay of Guayanilla, eastward of Guánica, and San German became the port of call for the Spanish ships bound to Pária. Its proximity to the "pearl coast," as the north shore of Venezuela was named, made it the point of departure for all who wished to reach that coast or escape from the shores of poverty-stricken Puerto Rico—namely, the dreamers of the riches of Peru, those who, like Sedeño, aspired to new conquests on the mainland, or crown officers who had good reasons for wishing to avoid giving an account of their administration of the royal revenues. The comparative prosperity which it enjoyed made San German the object of repeated attacks by the French privateers. It was burned and plundered several times during the forty-three years of its existence, till one day in September, 1554, three French ships of the line entered the port and landed a detachment of troops who plundered and destroyed everything to a distance of a league and a half into the interior. From that day San German, founded by Miguel del Torro, ceased to exist.

The town with the same name, existing at present on the southwest coast, was founded in 1570 by Governor Francisco Solis with the remains of the ill-fated settlement on the bay of Guayanilla. The Dominican friars had a large estate in this neighborhood, and the new settlement enhanced its value. Both the governor and the bishop were natives of Salamanca, and named the place New Salamanca, but the name of New San German has prevailed. In 1626 the new town had 50 citizens (vecinos).

San Juan.—Licentiate Velasquez, one of the king's officers at Capárra, wrote to his Highness in April, 1515: " ... The people of this town wish to move to an islet in the port. I went to see it with the town council and it looks well"; and some time later: " ... We will send a description of the islet to which it is convenient to remove the town of Puerto Rico."

Ponce opposed the change. His reasons were that the locality of Capárra was dry and level, with abundance of wood, water, and pasture, and that most of the inhabitants, occupied as they were with gold-washing, had to provide themselves with provisions from the neighboring granges. He recognized that the islet was healthier, but maintained that the change would benefit only the traders.

The dispute continued for some time. Medical certificates were presented declaring Capárra unhealthy. The leading inhabitants declared their opinion in favor of the transfer. A petition was signed and addressed to the Jerome friars, who governed in la Española, and they ordered the transfer in June, 1519. Ponce was permitted to remain in his stone house in the abandoned town as long as he liked. In November, 1520, Castro wrote to the emperor expressing his satisfaction with the change, and asked that a fort and a stone smelting-house might be constructed, because the one in use was of straw and had been burned on several occasions. Finally, in 1521, the translation of the capital of Puerto Rico to its present site was officially recognized and approved.

There were now two settlements in the island. There were 35 citizens in each in 1515, but the gold produced attracted others, and in 1529 the Bishop of la Española reported that there were 120 houses in San Juan, "some of stone, the majority of straw. The church was roofed while I was there." He says, "a Dominican monastery was in course of construction, nearly finished, with more than 125 friars in it."

During the next five years the gold produce rapidly diminished; the Indians, who extracted it, escaped or died. Tempests and epidemics devastated the land. The Caribs and the French freebooters destroyed what the former spared. All those who could, emigrated to Mexico or Peru, and such was the depopulated condition of the capital, that Governor Lando wrote in 1534: "If a ship with 50 men were to come during the night, they could land and kill all who live here."

With the inhabitants engaged in the cultivation of sugar-cane, some improvement in their condition took place. Still, there were only 130 citizens in San Juan in 1556, and only 30 in New San German. In 1595, when Drake appeared before San Juan with a fleet of 26 ships, the governor could only muster

126

a few peons and 50 horsemen, and but for the accidental presence of the Spanish frigates, Puerto Rico would probably be an English possession to-day. It *was* taken by the Duke of Cumberland four years later, but abandoned again on account of the epidemic that broke out among the English troops. When the Hollanders laid siege to the capital in 1625 there were only 330 men between citizens and jíbaros that could be collected for the defense. In 1646 there were 500 citizens and 400 houses in San Juan, and 200 citizens in New San German. Arecibo and Coámo had recently been founded.

Scarcely any progress in the settlement of the country was made during the remaining years of the seventeenth century. Toward the middle of the eighteenth century great steps in this direction had been made. From Governor Bravo de Rivera's list of men fit for militia service, we discover that in 1759 there were 18 new settlements or towns in the island with a total of 4,559 men able to carry arms; exclusive of San Juan and San German, they were:

Ponce with 356 men.
Aguáda with 564 "
Manatí " 357 "
Añasco " 460 "
Yauco " 164 "
Coámo " 342 "
La Tuna " 104 "
Arecibo " 647 "
Utuado " 126 "
Loiza " 179 "
Toa-Alta " 188 "
Toa-Baja " 294 "
Piedras " 104 "
Bayamón " 256 "
Cáguas " 100 "
Guayama " 211 "
Rio Piedras with 46 "
Cangrejos with 120 "

The oldest of these settlements is

La Aguáda.—The name signifies "place at which water is taken," and *Aguadilla*, which is to the north of the former and the head of the province, is merely the diminutive of Aguáda. The first possesses abundant springs of excellent water, one of them distant only five minutes from the landing-place. In Aguadilla a famous spring rises in the middle of the town and runs through it in a permanent stream.

In 1511 the king directed his officers in Seville to make all ships, leaving that port for the Indies, call at the island of San Juan in order to make the Caribs believe that the Spanish population was much larger than it really was, and thus prevent or diminish their attacks. The excellence of the water which the ships found at Aguáda made it convenient for them to call, and the Spanish ships continued to do so long after the need of frightening away the Caribs had passed.

The first regular settlement was founded in 1585 by the Franciscan monks, who named it San Francisco de Asis. The Caribs surprised the place about the year 1590, destroyed the convent, and martyrized five of the monks, which caused the temporary abandonment of the settlement. It was soon repeopled, notwithstanding the repeated attacks of Caribs and French and English privateers. Drake stopped there to provide his fleet with water in 1595. Cumberland did the same four years later. The Columbian insurgents attempted a landing in 1819 and another in 1825, but were beaten off. Their valiant conduct on these occasions, and their loyalty in contributing a large sum of money toward the expenses of the war in Africa, earned for their town, from the Home Government, the title of "unconquerable" (villa invicta) in 1860.

Aguáda, or rather the mouth of the river Culebrinas, which flows into the sea near it, is the place where Columbus landed in 1493. The fourth centenary of the event was commemorated in 1893 by the erection, on a granite pedestal, of a marble column, 11 meters high, crowned with a Latin cross. On the pedestal is the inscription:

1493

19th of November

1893

Loiza.—Along the borders of the river which bears this name there settled, about the year 1514, Pedro Mexia, Sancho Arángo, Francisco Quinaós, Pedro Lopez, and some other Spaniards, with their respective Indian laborers. In one of the raids of the Indians from Vieyques or Aye-Aye, which were so frequent at the time, a cacique named Cacimár met his death at the hands of Arángo. The fallen chief's brother Yaureibó, in revenge, prepared a large expedition, and penetrating at night with several pirogues full of men by way of the river to within a short distance of the settlement, fell upon it and utterly destroyed it, killing many and carrying off others. Among the killed were Mexia and his Indian concubine named Louisa or Heloise. Tradition says that this woman, having been advised by some Indian friend of the intended attack, tried to persuade her paramour to flee. When he refused, she scorned his recommendation to save herself and remained with him to share his fate.

In the relation of this episode by the chroniclers, figures also the name of the dog Becerrillo (small calf), a mastiff belonging to Arángo, who had brought the animal from the Española, where Columbus had introduced the breed on his second voyage. In the fight with the Indians Arángo was overpowered and was being carried off alive, when his dog, at the call of his master, came bounding to the rescue and made the Indians release him. They sprang into the river for safety, and the gallant brute following them was shot with a poisoned arrow.[82]

Arecibo is situated on the river of that name. It was founded by Felipe de Beaumont in 1616, with the appellation San Felipe de Arecibo.

Fajardo.—Governor Bravo de Rivero, with a view to found a settlement on the east coast, detached a number of soldiers from their regiment and gave to them and some other people a caballeria[83] of land each, in the district watered by the river Fajardo. Alexander O'Reilly, the king's commissioner, who visited the

128

settlement in 1765, found 474 people, and wrote: " ...They have cleared little ground and cultivated so little that they are still in the very commencements. The only industry practised by the inhabitants is illicit trade with the Danish islands of Saint Thomas and Saint Cross. The people of Fajardo are the commission agents for the people there. What else could be expected from indolent soldiers and vagabonds without any means of clearing forests or building houses? If no other measures are adopted this settlement will remain many years in the same unhappy condition and be useful only to foreigners." In 1780 there were 243 heads of families in the district; the town proper had 9 houses and a church.

With regard to the remaining settlements mentioned in Governor Bravo de Rivero's list, there are no reliable data.

From 1759, the year in which a general distribution of Government lands was practised and titles were granted, to the year 1774, in which Governor Miguel Muesas reformed or redistributed some of the urban districts, many, if not most of the settlements referred to were formed or received the names they bear at present.

FOOTNOTES:

[Footnote 81: The first landing of the American troops was effected here on July 25, 1898.]

[Footnote 82: These two episodes have given rise to several fantastic versions by native writers.]

[Footnote 83: Ten by twenty "cuerdas." The cuerda is one-tenth less than an English acre.]

CHAPTER XL
AURIFEROUS STREAMS AND GOLD PRODUCED FROM 1509 TO 1536

If a systematic exploration were practised to-day, by competent mineralogists, of the entire chain of mountains which intersects the island from east to west, it is probable that lodes of gold-bearing quartz or conglomerate, worth working, would be discovered. Even the alluvium deposits along the banks of the rivers and their tributaries, as well as the river beds, might, in many instances, be found to "pay."

The early settlers compelled the Indians to work for them. These poor creatures, armed with the simplest tools, dug the earth from the river banks. Their wives and daughters, standing up to their knees in the river, washed it in wooden troughs. When the output diminished another site was chosen, often before the first one was half worked out. The Indians' practical knowledge of the places where gold was likely to be found was the Spanish gold-seeker's only guide, the Indians' labor the only labor employed in the collection of it.

As for the mountains, they have never been properly explored. The Indians who occupied them remained in a state of insurrection for years, and when the mountain districts could be safely visited at last, the *auri sacra fames* had subsided. The governors did not interest themselves in the mineral resources of the island, and the people found it too difficult to provide for their daily wants to go prospecting. So the surface gold in the alluvium deposits was all that was collected by the Spaniards, and what there still may be on the bed-rocks of the rivers or in the lodes in the mountains from which it has been washed, awaits the advent of modern gold-seekers.

The first samples of gold from Puerto Rico were taken to the Española by Ponce, who had obtained them from the river Manatuabón, to which the friendly cacique Guaybána conducted him on his first visit (1508). This river disembogues into the sea on the south coast near Cape Malapascua; but it appears that the doughty captain also visited the north coast and found gold enough in the rivers Cóa and Sibúco to justify him in making his headquarters at Capárra, which is in the neighborhood. That gold was found there in considerable quantities is shown by the fact that in August of the same year of Ponce's return to the island (he returned in February, 1509), 8,975 pesos corresponded to the king's fifth of the first *washings*. The first *smelting* was practised October 26, 1510. The next occurred May 22, 1511, producing respectively 2,645 and 3,043 gold pesos as the king's share. Thus, in the three first years the crown revenues from this source amounted to 14,663 gold pesos, and the total output to 73,315 gold pesos, which, at three dollars of our money per peso, approximately represented a total of $219,945 obtained from the rivers in the neighborhood of Capárra alone.

In 1515 a fresh discovery of gold-bearing earth in this locality was reported to the king by Sancho Velasquez, the treasurer, who wrote on April 27th: " … At 4 leagues' distance from here rich gold deposits have been found in certain rivers and streams. From Reyes (December 4th) to March 15th, with very few Indians, 25,000 pesos have been taken out. It is expected that the output this season will be 100,000 pesos."

The streams in the neighborhood of San German, on the south coast, the only other settlement in the island at the time, seem to have been equally rich. The year after its foundation by Miguel del Toro the settlers were able to smelt and deliver 6,147 pesos to the royal treasurer. The next year the king's share amounted to 7,508 pesos, and Treasurer Haro reported that the same operation for the years 1517 and 1518 had produced $186,000 in all—that is, 3,740 for the treasury.

A good idea of the island's mineral and other resources at this period may be formed from Treasurer Haro's extensive report to the authorities in Madrid, dated January 21, 1518.

" … Your Highness's revenues," he says, "are: one-fifth of the gold extracted and of the pearls brought by those who go (to the coast of Venezuela) to purchase them, the salt produce and the duties on imports and exports. Every one of the three smeltings that are practised here every two years produces about 250,000 pesos, in San German about 186,000 pesos. But the amounts fluctuate.

"The product of pearls is uncertain. Since the advent of the Jerome fathers the business has been suspended until the arrival of your Highness. Two caravels have gone now, but few will go, because the fathers say that the traffic in Indians is to cease and the greatest profit is in that … On your Highness's estates there are 400 Indians who wash gold, work in the fields, build houses, etc.; … they produce from 1,500 to 2,000 pesos profit every gang (demora)…. I send in this ship, with

130

Juan Viscaino, 8,000 pesos and 40 marks of pearls. There remain in my possession 17,000 pesos and 70 marks of pearls, which shall be sent by the next ship in obedience to your Highness's orders, not to send more than 10,000 pesos at a time. The pearls that go now are worth that amount. Until the present we sent only 5,000 pesos' worth of pearls at one time."

The yearly output of gold fluctuated, but it continued steadily, as Velasquez wrote to the emperor in 1521, when he made a remittance of 5,000 pesos. Six or seven years later, the placers, for such they were, were becoming exhausted. Castellanos, the treasurer, wrote in 1518 that only 429 pesos had been received as the king's share of the last two years' smelting. Some new deposit was discovered in the river Daguáo, but it does not seem to have been of much importance. From the year 1530 the reports of the crown officers are full of complaints of the growing scarcity of gold; finally, in 1536, the last remittance was made; not, it may be safely assumed, because there was no more gold in the island, but because those who had labored and suffered in its production, had succumbed to the unaccustomed hardships imposed on them and to the cruel treatment received from their sordid masters.

Besides the river mentioned, the majority of those which have their sources in the mountains of Luquillo are more or less auriferous. These are: the Rio Prieto, the Fajardo, the Espíritu Santo, the Rio Grande, and, especially, the Mameyes. The river Loiza also contains gold, but, judging from the traces of diggings still here and there visible along the beds of the Mavilla, the Sibúco, the Congo, the Rio Negro, and Carozal, in the north, it would seem that these rivers and their affluents produced the coveted metal in largest quantities. The Duey, the Yauco, and the Oromico, or Hormigueros, on the south coast are supposed to be auriferous also, but do not seem to have been worked.

The metal was and is still found in seed-shaped grains, sometimes of the weight of 2 or 3 pesos. Tradition speaks of a nugget found in the Fajardo river weighing 4 ounces, and of another found in an affluent of the Congo of 1 pound in weight.

Silver.—In 1538 the crown officers in San Juan wrote to the Home Government: " ... The gold is diminishing. Several veins of lead ore have been discovered, from which some silver has been extracted. The search would continue if the concession to work these veins were given for ten years, with 1.20 or 1.15 royalty." On March 29th of the following year the same officers reported: " ... Respecting the silver ores discovered, we have smolten some, but no one here knows how to do it. Veins of this ore have been discovered in many parts of the island, but nobody works them. We are waiting for some one to come who knows how to smelt them."

The following extract from the memoirs and documents left by Juan Bautista Muñoz, gives the value in "gold pesos"[84] of the bullion and pearls, corresponding to the king's one-fifth share of the total produce remitted to Spain from this island from the year 1509 to 1536:

In 1509, gold pesos 8,975
1510, " 2,645

1511, " 10,000
1512, " 3,043
1513, " 27,291
1514, " 18,000
1515, " 17,000
1516, " 11,490
1517-18, " 38,497
1519, " 10,000
1520, " 35,733
In 1521, " 10,000
1522, " 7,979
1523-29, " 40,000
1530, " 12,440
1531, " 6,500
1532, " 9,000
1533, " 4,000
1534, " 8,500
1535, " 1,848
1536, " 10,000

Total, 15 share 277,941

The entire output for this period was 1,389,705 gold pesos, or $4,169,115 Spanish coin of to-day, as the total produce in gold and pearls of the island of San Juan de Puerto Rico during the first twenty-seven years of its occupation by the Spaniards.

FOOTNOTES:

[Footnote 84: Washington Irving estimates the value of the "gold peso" of the sixteenth century at $3 Spanish money of our day.]

CHAPTER XLI
WEST INDIAN HURRICANES IN PUERTO RICO FROM 1515 TO 1899

Whoever has witnessed the awful magnificence of what the primitive inhabitants of the West Indian islands called *ou-ra-cán,* will never forget the sense of his own utter nothingness and absolute helplessness. With the wind rushing at the rate of 65 or more miles an hour, amid the roar of waves lashed into furious rolling mountains of water, the incessant flash of lightning, the dreadful roll of thunder, the fierce beating of rain, one sees giant trees torn up by the roots and man's proud constructions of stone and iron broken and scattered like children's toys.

The tropical latitudes to the east and north of the West Indian Archipelago are the birthplace of these phenomena. According to Mr. Redfield[85] they cover simultaneously an extent of surface from 100 to 500 miles in diameter, acting with diminished violence toward the circumference and with increased energy toward the center of this space.

132

In the Weather Bureau's bulletin cited, there is a description of the most remarkable and destructive among the 355 hurricanes that have swept over the West Indies from 1492 to 1899. Not a single island has escaped the tempest's ravages. I have endeavored in vain to make an approximate computation of the human life and property destroyed by these visitations of Providence. Such a computation is impossible when we read of entire towns destroyed not once but 6, 8, and 10 times; of crops swept away by the tempest's fury, and the subsequent starvation of untold thousands; of whole fleets of ships swallowed up by the sea with every soul on board, and of hundreds of others cast on shore like coco shards.

To give an idea of the appalling disasters caused by these too oft recurring phenomena, the above-mentioned bulletin gives Flammarion's description of the great hurricane of 1780.[86]

"The most terrible cyclone of modern times is probably that which occurred on October 10, 1780, which has been specially called the great hurricane, and which seems to have embodied all the horrible scenes that attend a phenomenon of this kind. Starting from Barbados, where trees and houses were all blown down, it engulfed an English fleet anchored before St. Lucia, and then ravaged the whole of that island, where 6,000 persons were buried beneath the ruins. From thence it traveled to Martinique, overtook a French transport fleet and sunk 40 ships conveying 4,000 soldiers. The vessels *disappeared*."

Such is the laconic language in which the governor reported the disaster. Farther north, Santo Domingo, St. Vincent, St. Eustatius, and Puerto Rico were devastated, and most of the vessels that were sailing in the track of the cyclone were lost with all on board. Beyond Puerto Rico the tempest turned northeast toward Bermuda, and though its violence gradually decreased, it nevertheless sunk several English vessels. This hurricane was quite as destructive inland. Nine thousand persons perished in Martinique, and 1,000 in St. Pierre, where not a single house was left standing, for the sea rose to a height of 25 feet, and 150 houses that were built along the shore were engulfed. At Port Royal the cathedral, 7 churches, and 1,400 houses were blown down; 1,600 sick and wounded were buried beneath the ruins of the hospital. At St. Eustatius, 7 vessels were dashed to pieces on the rocks, and of the 19 which lifted their anchors and went out to sea, only 1 returned. At St. Lucia the strongest buildings were torn up from their foundations, a cannon was hurled a distance of more than 30 yards, and men as well as animals were lifted off their feet and carried several yards. The sea rose so high that it destroyed the fort and drove a vessel against the hospital with such force as to stave in the walls of that building. Of the 600 houses at Kingston, on the island of St. Vincent, 14 alone remained intact, and the French frigate Junon was lost. Alarming consequences were feared from the number of dead bodies which lay uninterred, and the quantity of fish the sea threw up, but these alarms soon subsided...."

"The aboriginal inhabitants," says Abbad, "foresaw these catastrophes two or three days in advance. They were sure of their approach when they perceived a hazy atmosphere, the red aspect of the sun, a dull, rumbling, subterranean sound, the stars shining through a kind of mist which made them look larger, the nor'west horizon heavily clouded, a strong-smelling emanation from the sea, a heavy swell with calm weather, and sudden changes of the wind from east to west." The Spanish settlers also learned to foretell the approach of a hurricane by the sulphurous exhalations of the earth, but especially by the incessant neighing of horses, bellowing of cattle, and general restlessness of these animals, who seem to acquire a presentiment of the coming danger.

"The physical features of hurricanes are well understood. The approach of a hurricane is usually indicated by a long swell on the ocean, propagated to great distances, and forewarning the observer by two or three days. A faint rise in the barometer occurs before the gradual fall, which becomes very pronounced at the center. Fine wisps of cirrus-clouds are first seen, which surround the center to a distance of 200 miles; the air is calm and sultry, but this is gradually supplanted by a gentle breeze, and later the wind increases to a gale, the clouds become matted, the sea rough, rain falls, and the winds are gusty and dangerous as the vortex comes on. Then comes the indescribable tempest, dealing destruction, impressing the imagination with the wild exhibition of the forces of nature, the flashes of lightning, the torrents of rain, the cold air, all the elements in an uproar, which indicate the close approach of the center. In the midst of this turmoil there is a sudden pause, the winds almost cease, the sky clears, the waves, however, rage in great turbulence. This is the eye of the storm, the core of the vortex, and it is, perhaps, 20 miles in diameter, or one-thirtieth of the whole hurricane. The respite is brief, and is soon followed by the abrupt renewal of the violent wind and rain, but now coming from the opposite direction, and the storm passes off with the several features following each other in the reverse order." [87]

The distribution over the months of the year of the 355 West Indian hurricanes which occurred during the four hundred and six years elapsed since the discovery, to the last on the list, is as follows:

Months. No of hurricanes.

January 5
February 7
March 11
April 6
May 5
June 10
July 42
August 96
September 80
October 69
November 17
December 7
  355

Puerto Rico has been devastated by hurricanes more than 20 times since its occupation by the Spaniards. But the records, beyond the mere statement of the facts, are very incomplete. Four stand out prominently as having committed terrible ravages. These are the hurricanes of Santa Ana, on July 26, 1825; Los Angeles, on August 2,1837; San Narciso, on October 29, 1867, and San Ciriaco, on August 8, 1899.

The first mention of the occurrence of a hurricane in this island we find in a letter from the crown officers to the king, dated August 8, 1515, wherein they explain: " ... In these last smeltings there was little gold, because many Indians died in consequence of sickness caused by the tempest as well as from want of food ..."

The next we read of was October 8, 1526, and is thus described by licentiate Juan de Vadillo:

"On the night of the 4th of October last there broke over this island such a violent storm of wind and rain, which the natives call '*ou-ra-cán*' that it destroyed the greater part of this city (San Juan) with the church. In the country it caused such damage by the overflow of rivers that many rich men have been made poor."

On September 8, 1530, Governor Francisco Manuel de Lando reported to the king: "During the last six weeks there have been three storms of wind and rain in this island (July 26, August 23 and 31). They have destroyed all the plantations, drowned many cattle, and caused much hunger and misery in the land. In this city the half of the houses were entirely destroyed, and of the other half the least injured is without a roof. In the country and in the mines nothing has remained standing. Everybody is ruined and thinking of going away."

1537.—July and August. The town officers wrote to the king in September: "In the last two months we have had three storms of wind and rain, the greatest that have been seen in this island, and as the plantations are along the banks of the rivers the floods have destroyed them all. Many slaves and cattle have been drowned, and this has caused much discouragement among the settlers, who before were inclined to go away, and are now more so."

1575.—September 21 (San Mateo), hurricane mentioned in the memoirs of Father Torres Vargas.

1614.—September 12, mentioned by the same chronicler in the following words: "Fray Pedro de Solier came to his bishopric in the year 1615, the same in which a great tempest occurred, after more than forty years since the one called of San Mateo. This one happened on the 12th of September. It did so much damage to the cathedral that it was necessary partly to cover it with straw and write to his Majesty asking for a donation to repair it. With his accustomed generosity he gave 4,000 ducats."

1678.—Abbad states that a certain Count or Duke Estren, an English commander, with a fleet of 22 ships and a body of landing troops appeared before San Juan and demanded its surrender, but that, before the English had time to land, a violent hurricane occurred which stranded every one of the British ships on Bird Island. Most of the people on board perished, and the few who saved their lives were made prisoners of war.

1740.—Precise date unknown. Monsieur Moreau de Jonnès, in his work,[88] says that this hurricane destroyed a coco-palm grove of 5 or 6 leagues in extent, which existed near Ponce. Other writers confirm this.

1772, August 28.—Friar Iñigo Abbad, who was in the island at the time, gives the following description of this tempest: "About a quarter to eleven of the night of the 28th of August the storm began to be felt in the capital of the island. A dull but continuous roll of thunder filled the celestial hemisphere, the sound as of approaching torrents of rain, the frightful sight of incessant lightning, and a slow quaking of the earth accompanied the furious wind. The tearing up of trees, the lifting of roofs, smashing of windows, and leveling of everything added terror-striking noises to the scene. The tempest raged with the same fury in the capital till after one o'clock in the morning. In other parts of the island it began about the same hour, but without any serious effect till later. In Aguáda, where I was at the time, nothing was felt till half-past two in the morning. It blew violently till a quarter to four, and the wind continued, growing less strong, till noon. During this time the wind came from all points of the compass, and the storm visited every part of the island, causing more damage in some places than others, according to their degree of exposure."

1780, June 13, and 1788, August 16.—No details of these two hurricanes are found in any of the Puerto Rican chronicles.

1804, September 4.—A great cyclone, a detailed description of which is given in the work of Mr. Jonnés.

1818 and 1814—Both hurricanes happened on the same date, that is, the 23d of July. Yauco and San German suffered most. A description of the effects of these storms was given in the Dario Económico of the 11th of August, 1814.

1819, September 21.—(San Mateo.) This cyclone is mentioned by Jonnés and by Córdova, who says that it caused extraordinary damages on the plantations.

1825, July 26.—(Santa Ana.) Córdova (vol. ii, p. 21 of his Memoirs) says of this hurricane: "It destroyed the towns of Patillas, Maunabó, Yabucóa, Humacáo, Gurabó, and Cáguas. In the north, east, and center of the island it caused great damage. More than three hundred people and a large number of cattle perished; 500 persons were badly wounded. The rivers rose to an unheard of extent, and scarcely a house remained standing. In the capital part of the San Antonio bridge was blown down, and the city wall facing the Marina on Tanca Creek was cracked. The royal Fortaleza (the present Executive Mansion) suffered much, also the house of Ponce. The lightning-conductors of the powder-magazine were blown down."

1837, August 2.—(Los Angeles.) This cyclone was general over the island and caused exceedingly grave losses of life and property. All the ships in the harbor of San Juan were lost.

1840, September 16.—No details.

1851, August 18.—No details, except that this hurricane caused considerable damage.

1867, October 29.—(San Narciso.) No details.

1871, August 23.—(San Felipe.) No details. *1899, August 8.*—(San Ciriaco.) When this hurricane occurred there was a meteorological station in operation in San Juan, and we are therefore enabled to present the following data from Mr. Geddings's report: "The rainfall was excessive, as much as 23 inches falling at

136

Adjuntas during the course of twenty-four hours. This caused severe inundations of rivers, and the deaths from drowning numbered 2,569 as compared with 800 killed by injuries received from the effects of the wind. This number does not include the thousands who have since died from starvation. The total loss of property was 35,889,013 pesos."

The United States Government and people promptly came to the assistance of the starving population, and something like 32,000,000 rations were distributed by the army during the ten months succeeding the hurricane.

* * * * *

Such are the calamities that are suspended over the heads of the inhabitants of the West Indian Islands. From July to October, at any moment, the sapphire skies may turn black with thunder-clouds; the Eden-like landscapes turned into scenes of ruin and desolation; the rippling ocean that lovingly laves their shores becomes a roaring monster trying to swallow them. The refreshing breezes that fan them become a destructive blast. Yet, such is the fecundity of nature in these regions that a year after a tempest has swept over an island, if the debris be removed, not a trace of its passage is visible—the fields are as green as ever, the earth, the trees, and plants that were spared by the tempest double their productive powers as if to indemnify the afflicted inhabitants for the losses they suffered.

FOOTNOTES:

[Footnote 85: See Bulletin H, Weather Bureau, West Indian Hurricanes, by E.B. Garriott, Washington, 1900.]

[Footnote 86: L'Atmosphère, p. 377 and following.]

[Footnote 87: Enrique del Monte, Havana University, On the Climate of the West Indies and West Indian Hurricanes.]

[Footnote 88: Histoire physique des Antilles Françaises.]

CHAPTER XLII
THE CARIBS

The origin of the Caribs, their supposed cannibalism and other customs have occasioned much controversy among West Indian chroniclers. The first question is undecided, and probably will remain so forever. With regard to cannibalism, in spite of the confirmative assurances of the early Spanish chroniclers, we have the testimony of eminent authorities to the contrary; and the writings of Jesuit missionaries who have lived many years among the Caribs give us a not unfavorable idea of their character and social institutions.

The first European who became intimately acquainted with the people of the West Indian Islands, on the return from his first voyage, wrote to the Spanish princes: " ... In all these islands I did not observe much difference in the faces and figures of the inhabitants, nor in their customs, nor in their language, seeing that they all understand each other, which is very singular." On the other hand the readiness with which the inhabitants of Aye-Aye and the other Carib islands gave asylum to the fugitive Boriquén Indians and joined them in their retaliatory expeditions, also points to the existence of some bond of kinship between them, so that there is ground for the opinion entertained by some writers that all the inhabitants of all the Antilles were of the race designated under the generic name of Caribs.

The theory generally accepted at first was, that at the time of the discovery two races of different origin occupied the West Indian Archipelago. The larger Antilles with the groups of small islands to the north of them were supposed to be inhabited by a race named Guaycures, driven from the peninsula of Florida by the warlike Seminoles; the Guaycures, it is said, could easily have reached the Bahamas and traversed the short distance that separated them from Cuba in their canoes, some of which could contain 100 men, and once there they would naturally spread over the neighboring islands. It is surmised that they occupied them at the time of the advent of the Phoenicians in this hemisphere, and Dr. Calixto Romero, in an interesting article on Lucúo, the god of the Boriquéns,[89] mentions a tradition referring to the arrival of these ancient navigators, and traces some of the Boriquén religious customs to them. The Guaycures were a peacefully disposed race, hospitable, indolent, fond of dancing and singing, by means of which they transmitted their legends from generation to generation. They fell an easy prey to the Spaniards. Velasquez conquered Cuba without the loss of a man. Juan Esquivél made himself master of Jamaica with scarcely any sacrifice, and if the aborigines of the Española and Boriquén resisted, it was only after patiently enduring insupportable oppression for several years.

The other race which inhabited the Antilles were said to have come from the south. They were supposed to have descended the Orinoco, spreading along the shore of the continent to the west of the river's mouths and thence to have invaded one after the other all the lesser Antilles. They were in a fair way of occupying the larger Antilles also when the discoveries of Columbus checked their career.

In support of the theory of the south-continental origin of the Caribs we have, in the first place, the work of Mr. Aristides Rojas on Venezuelan hieroglyphics, wherein he treats of numerous Carib characters on the rocks along the plains and rivers of that republic, marking their itinerary from east to west. He states that the Acháguas, the aboriginals of Columbia, gave to these wanderers, on account of their ferocity, the name of Chabi-Nabi, that is, tiger-men or descendants of tigers.

In the classification of native tribes in Codazzi's geography of Venezuela, he includes the Caribs, and describes them as "a very numerous race, enterprising and warlike, which in former times exercised great influence over the whole territory extending from Ecuador to the Antilles. They were the tallest and most robust Indians known on the continent; they traded in slaves, and though they were cruel and ferocious in their incursions, they were not cannibals like their kinsmen of the lesser Antilles, who were so addicted to the custom of eating their prisoners that the names of cannibal and Carib had become synonymous." [90]

Another theory of the origin of the Caribs is that advanced by M. d'Orbigny, who, after eight years of travel over the South American continent, published the result of his researches in Paris in 1834. He considers them to be a branch of the great Guaraní family. And the Jesuit missionaries, Fathers Raymond and Dutertre, who lived many years among the Antillean Caribs, concluded from their traditions

138

that they were descended from a people on the continent named Galibis, who, according to M. d'Orbigny, were a branch of the Guaranís.

But the Guaranís, though a very wide-spread family of South American aborigines, were neither a conquering nor a wandering race. They occupied that part of the continent situated between the rivers Paraguay and Paraná, from where these two rivers join the river Plate, northward, to about latitude 22° south. This region was the home of the Guaranís, a people indolent, sensual, and peaceful, among whom the Jesuits, in the eighteenth century founded a religious republic, which toward the end of that period counted 33 towns with a total population of over one hundred thousand souls. A glance at the map will show the improbability of any Indian tribe, no matter how warlike, making its way from the heart of the continent to the Orinoco through 30° of primitive forests, mountains, and rivers, inhabited by hostile tribes.[91]

The French missionaries who lived many years with the Caribs of Guadeloupe and the other French possessions, do not agree on the subject of their origin. Fathers Dutertre and Raymond believe them to be the descendants of the Galibis, a people inhabiting Guiana. Fathers Rochefort, Labat, and Bristol maintain that they are descended from the Apalaches who inhabited the northern part of Florida. Humboldt is of the same opinion, and suggests that the name Carib may be derived from Calina or Caripuna through transformation of the letters *l* and *p* into *r* and *b*, forming Caribi or Galibi.[92] Pedro Martyr strongly opposes this opinion, the principal objection to which is that a tribe from the North American continent invading the West Indies by way of Florida would naturally occupy the larger Antilles before traveling east and southward. Under this hypothesis, as we have said, all the inhabitants of the Antilles would be Caribs, but in that case the difference in the character of the inhabitants of the two divisions of the archipelago would have to be accounted for.

Most of the evidence we have been able to collect on this subject points to a south-continental origin of the Caribs. On the maps of America, published in 1587 by Abraham Ortellus, of Antwerp, in 1626 by John Speed, of London, and in 1656 by Sanson d'Abbeville in Paris, the whole region to the north of the Orinoco is marked Caribana. In the history of the Dutch occupation of Guiana we read that hostile Caribs occupied a shelter[93] constructed in 1684 by the governor on the borders of the Barima, which shows that the vast region along the Orinoco and its tributaries, as well as the lesser Antilles, was inhabited by an ethnologically identical race.

* * * * *

Were the Caribs cannibals? This question has been controverted as much as that of their origin, and with the same doubtful result.

The only testimony upon which the assumption that the Caribs were cannibals is founded is that of the companions of Columbus on his second voyage, when, landing at Guadeloupe, they found human bones and skulls in the deserted huts. No other evidence of cannibalism of a positive character was ever after obtained, so that the belief in it rests exclusively upon Chanca's narrative of what the Spaniards saw and learned during the few days of their stay among the islands.

Their imagination could not but be much excited by the sight of what the doctor describes as "infinite quantities" of bones of human creatures, who, they took for granted, had been devoured, and of skulls hanging on the walls by way of receptacles for curios. It was the age of universal credulity, and for more than a century after the most absurd tales with regard to the people and things of the mysterious new continent found ready credence even among men of science. Columbus, in his letter to Santangel (February, 1493), describing the different islands and people, wrote: "I have not yet seen any of the human monsters that are supposed to exist here." The descriptions of the customs of the natives of the newly discovered islands which Dr. Chanca sent to the town council of Seville were unquestioned by them, and afterward by the Spanish chroniclers; but there is reason to believe with Mr. Ignacio Armas, an erudite Cuban author, who published a paper in 1884 entitled the Fable of the Caribs, that the belief in their cannibalism originated in an error of judgment, was an illusion afterward, and ended by being a calumny[97]. Father Bartolomé de las Casas was the first to contradict this belief. "They [the Spaniards] saw skulls," he says, "and human bones. These must have been of chiefs or other persons whom they held in esteem, because, to say that they were the remains of people who had been eaten, if the natives devoured as many as was supposed, the houses could not contain the bones, and there is no reason why, after eating them, they should preserve the relics. All this is but guesswork." Washington Irving agrees with the reverend historian, and describes the general belief in the cannibalism of the Caribs to the Spaniards' fear of them. Two eminent authorities positively deny it. Humboldt, in his before-cited work, in the chapter on Carib missions, says: "All the missionaries of the Carony, of the lower Orinoco, and of the plains of Cari, whom we have had occasion to consult, have assured us that the Caribs were perhaps the least anthropophagous of any tribes on the new continent, ..." and Sir Robert Schomburgh, who was charged by the Royal Geographical Society with the survey of Guiana in 1835, reported that among the Caribs he found peace and contentment, simple family affections, and frank gratitude for kindness shown. [94]

* * * * *

The narratives of the French, English, and Dutch conquerors of the Guianas and the lesser Antilles accord with the observations of Humboldt in describing the Caribs as an ambitious and intelligent race, among whom there still existed traces of a superior social organization, such as the hereditary power of chiefs, respect for the priestly caste, and attachment to ancient customs. Employed only in fishing and hunting, the Carib was accustomed to the use of arms from childhood; war was the principal object of his existence, and the proofs through which the young warrior had to pass before being admitted to the ranks of the braves, remind us of the customs of certain North American Indians.

They were of a light yellow color with a sooty tint, small, black eyes, white and well-formed teeth, straight, shining, black hair, without a beard or hair on any other part of their bodies. The expression of their face was sad, like that of all savage tribes in tropical regions. They were of middle size, but strong and

140

vigorous. To protect their bodies from the stings of insects they anointed them with the juice or oil of certain plants. They were polygamous. From their women they exacted the most absolute submission. The females did all the domestic labor, and were not permitted to eat in the presence of the men. In case of infidelity the husband had the right to kill his wife. Each family formed a village by itself (carbet) where the oldest member ruled.

Their industry, besides the manufacture of their arms and canoes, was limited to the spinning and dyeing of cotton goods, notably their hammocks, and the making of pottery for domestic uses. Though possessing no temples, nor religious observances, they recognized two principles or spirits, the spirit of good (boyee) and the spirit of evil (maboya). The priests invoked the first or drove out the second as occasion required. Each individual had his good spirit.

Their language resembled in sound the Italian, the words being sonorous, terminating in vowels. By the end of the eighteenth century the missionaries had made vocabularies of 50 Carib dialects, and the Bible had been translated into one of them, the Arawak. A remarkable custom was the use of two distinct languages, one by the males, another by the females. Tradition says that when the Caribs first invaded the Antilles they put to death all the males but spared the females. The women continued speaking their own tongue and taught it to their daughters, but the sons learned their fathers' language. In time, both males and females learned both languages.

"It is true," says the Jesuit Father Rochefort, in his Histoire des Antilles, "that the Caribs have degenerated from the virtues of their ancestors, but it is also true that the Europeans, by their pernicious examples, their ill-treatment of them, their villainous deceit, their dastardly breaking of every promise, their pitiless plundering and burning of their villages, their beastly violation of their girls and women, have taught them, to the eternal infamy of the name of Christian, to lie, to betray, to be licentious, and other vices which they knew not before they came in contact with us."

Father Dutertre declares that at the time of the arrival of the Europeans the Caribs were contented, happy, and sociable. Physically they were the best made and healthiest people of America. Theft was unknown to them, nothing was hidden; their huts had neither doors nor windows, and when, after the advent of the French, a Carib missed anything in his hut, he used to say: "A Christian has been here!" Dutertre says that in thirty-five years all the French missionaries together, by taking the greatest pains, had not been able to convert 20 adults. Those who were thought to have embraced Christianity returned to their practises as soon as they rejoined their fellows. "The reason for this want of success," says the father, "is the bad impression produced on the minds of these intelligent natives by the cruelties and immoralities of the Christians, which are more barbarous than those of the islanders themselves. They have inspired the Caribs with such a horror of Christianity that the greatest reproach they can think of for an enemy is to call him a Christian."

The reason the Spaniards never attempted the conquest of the Caribs is clear. There was no gold in their islands. They defended their homes foot by foot, and if, by chance, they were taken prisoners, they preferred suicide to slavery. Toward the end of the eighteenth century there still existed a few hundred of the race in the island of St. Vincent. They were known as the black Caribs, because they were largely mixed with fugitive negro slaves from other islands and with the people of a slave-ship wrecked on their coast in 1685. They lived there tranquil and isolated till 1795, when the island was settled by French colonists, and they were finally absorbed by them. They were the last representatives in the Antilles of a race which, during five centuries, had ruled both on land and sea. On the continent, along the Esequibo and its affluents, they are numerous still; but in their contact with the European settlers in those regions they have lost the strength and the virtues of their former state without acquiring those of the higher civilization. Like all aboriginals under similar conditions, they are slowly disappearing.

FOOTNOTES:

[Footnote 89: Revista Puertoriqueña, Tomo I, Año I, 1887.]

[Footnote 90: The word "cannibal" is but a corruption of guaribó, is, "brave or strong," changed into Caribó, Caríba, and finally that Carib. The name Galibi, also applied to the Caribs, means equally strong or brave.]

[Footnote 91: The author visited this region and sketched some of the ruins of these Jesuit-Guarani missions, of which scarcely one stone has remained on the other. They were destroyed by the Brazilians after the suppression of the Society of Jesus by Pope Clement XIV in 1773; the defenseless Indians were cruelly butchered or carried off as slaves. The sculptured remains of temples, of gardens and orchards grown into jungles still attest the high degree of development attained by these missions under the guidance of the Jesuit fathers.]

[Footnote 92: Voyage aux Regions Equinoctiales du Nouveau Continent, Paris, 1826.]

[Footnote 93: "Kleyn pleysterhuisye," small plaster house.]

[Footnote 94: As an example of the credulity of the people of the period, see Theodore Bry's work in the library of Congress in Washington, in which there is a map of Guiana, published in Frankfort in 1599. On it are depicted with short descriptions the lake of Parmié and the city of Manáo, which represent El Dorado, in search of which hundreds of Spaniards and thousands of Indians lost their lives. There is a picture of one of the Amazons, with a short notice of their habits and customs, and there is the portrait of one of the inhabitants of the country Twai-Panoma, who were born without heads, but had eyes, nose, and mouth conveniently located in their breast.]

Made in the USA
Lexington, KY
07 December 2019

58263155R00079